RUNNING WITH

RUNNING
with the
KRAYS

MY LIFE IN LONDON'S GANGLAND

BILLY WEBB

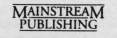

MAINSTREAM
PUBLISHING
EDINBURGH AND LONDON

FORGOTTEN MEN

This book is dedicated to Ginger Marks, Jackie Frost, Teddy Smith and the many others who vanished from the face of the earth during the Krays' reign, and who are still on Scotland Yard's missing persons list. Had Ronnie Kray had his way, my brother Ron and I would be on that list.

Copyright © Billy Webb, 1993
All rights reserved
The moral right of the author has been asserted

First published in Great Britain in 1993 by
MAINSTREAM PUBLISHING COMPANY (EDINBURGH) LTD
7 Albany Street
Edinburgh EH1 3UG

This edition 1995
Reprinted 1997

ISBN 1 85158 769 1

A catalogue record for this book is available from the British Library

Typeset in Palatino by Litho Link Ltd, Welshpool, Powys, Wales
Printed and bound in Great Britain by
Caledonian International Book Manufacturing Ltd, Glasgow

Contents

Introduction

There's a good chance that sometime in the next year the Krays might be unleashed on London again. There's a campaign to have them released, but the public have forgotten the relief they felt when the twins were put away. They've forgotten that George Cornell was shot dead in a pub in front of witnesses who were too terrified to come forward, and they've forgotten that Jack 'The Hat' McVitie was murdered for no other reason than that he had annoyed Ronnie Kray.

The Krays' reign of terror was based on nothing but cowardice. They wanted to be kings of all they surveyed but they were kings of nothing but bloodshed. Their attempts to deceive the public included trying to hire top publicity men to project the right image. They even tried to get Brian Epstein, the Beatles manager, to glamorise them. Photos taken by David Bailey were on sale for 3/6d in Soho. And now there are television programmes about how they have paid their debt to society.

The Kray twins have fooled the public into seeing them as a couple of Robin Hoods and the result is a Ronnie and Reggie Kray industry. They have a well-organised marketing set-up run by Peter Gillette who Reggie met in prison and who later went back in after adding drugs to his marketing activities. Under Peter Gillette's management the twins have made a fortune from Parkhurst and Broadmoor. There is a Kray record album with songs supposedly written by Reggie and there are books which they are supposed to have written themselves which are best-sellers. There are Kray T-shirts and a line in signed coloured prints of the twins selling at £150 each. By 1990 alone the books were reputed to have made £20,000, the prints £300,000 and the T-shirts £20,000. The film about their lives which glamorised them made them another £160,000. The latest racket is The Kray Supporters Club that cons the lunatic fringe into paying £12.99 a year for a quarterly newsletter with a pen-pal section. According to the Kray publicity machine, some of the profits of all these scams are given to charity.

While the twins have been paying their debt to society for their years of killing and maiming they have stashed away a fortune. I have written this book to expose the other side of the myth that has been built up around them over the years. I first met the Krays when we were teenagers. Then we became fugitives when we were all deserters from the army. At the time they seemed very confused about how to survive. But from then on the pattern of my life frequently criss-crossed the gory tale of Reggie and Ronnie Kray.

I have been involved in many aspects of the protection game one way or another for many years. I have had to carry weapons to protect myself and I have used them as well as having them used on me. But I have never performed violence just for kicks, the way the Krays did. I have never encouraged the people I worked alongside to shed blood just for the sake of being able to say, 'I did it.' Although I do not see myself as a saint, I believe the Krays have a basic evil embedded in their personalities, which I have not. In my career I have used weapons against people and if I were shot dead or beaten to death tomorrow, as I could be, my former acts of violence would exonerate my killers and the police would breathe a sigh of relief.

I am writing this book because I think people need reminding of the sort of people the Kray twins are – and how they managed to attract a kind of glamour to their deeds by being photographed with celebrities like Judy Garland, George Raft, Joe Louis, Sophie Tucker, Diana Dors, Barbra Streisand and Billy Daniels, as well as politicians like Tom Driberg and Lord Boothby. Somehow they made ordinary people believe that they needed sympathy for being the way they are, rather than needing to be locked away where they can do no more damage. Even the film about them, which was supposed to be a truthful story of their lives, tried to show them as a couple of nice guys who had some minor personality problems. It managed to both glamorise their misdeeds and misrepresent them as a kind of East End homestead cottage industry.

In their book, *Our Story*, they say what nice people they really are. They say that their mother brought them up with a strong sense of moral values, and that they are really gentlemen, but that the police needed them as scapegoats. Make no mistake, the Kray twins ruled London with a combination of violence and terror. They were not courageous in the way they did this. They could not stand up for themselves without the backing of their gang of toughs and stooges. The killings they carried out were done for show – planned and executed in a way that made sure they could kill with hardly any risk to their own persons. Despite the long period they have been locked away neither of them has ever expressed the slightest remorse, except when Ronnie told a reporter who interviewed him in Broadmoor: 'The murders we did were ordinary murders of people from gangland. We didn't do any kids or old ladies.'

I have letters from them describing their plans on their release to open a gambling club called Sweeney Todd's. They want to have the floors covered in sawdust, looking as if stained with blood. This is not the talk of men who are sorry for the killings they've done and want to lead a lawful life after taking their punishment.

Before they were locked up for murder there was a period when London's clubland didn't know what hit it. The Krays moved in and took over wherever they could. If anyone opened a club or spieler (gambling club) anywhere near a Kray establishment the

Krays went in and said: 'Listen. You've opened near us so we want a share.' And they'd get it. If they didn't, their victim would pay in another way. Just to say the name 'Kray' was enough to arouse fear and terror in people in those days.

After the longest criminal trial in British history the twins were given life, with a minimum of 30 years. The judge said society needed a long rest from them. I say we need a longer one than the twins are planning at the moment.

Let's thank God (or whoever) that the Kray twins never reproduced themselves. It's a strange thing when you look back at all the evil bastards in history. Many never reproduced themselves – had children, that is: Myra Hindley, Ian Brady, The Yorkshire Ripper, Donald Neilson, Reginald Christie, Haigh, Heath. I am glad to say I have fathered two children and have only been involved in organised crime for the money, not for the opportunity to smash other people's lives.

When you have known people for 40 years, as I've known the Krays, and lived with them in various flats and rooms and spent night after night in all-night cafes and sleazy clubs and spielers, drinking endless cups of coffee and constantly taking benzedrine, dexedrine and so on to stay awake, and when you have spent month after month, amounting to many years, as a fugitive from the police and the army with them, only then can you lay claim to knowing people. With the Krays, fate decided that our paths would cross a hundred times or more as friends and foes from when we were teenagers to being middle-aged.

I believe it's morally wrong that society concentrates on the Krays to the exclusion of their victims. It's wrong that the Krays are built up as celebrities and heroes. This just encourages the lunatic fringe to follow the Krays' example and seek out and even kill innocent victims in order to achieve immortality.

Last but not least, the Krays' present followers – fans, supporters or whatever – never knew them during their reign but are now crying out for sympathy for two murderers. When did the Krays ever show sympathy to any of their victims? And how would any of the Kray fans feel if one of their loved ones was a victim of the Kray murder machine? They should spare some thought for the feelings of the relations of the Kray victims who are now having to put up with the glamorisation of the Kray twins, whilst their loved ones lay silent in their graves.

CHAPTER ONE

'I Could Use a Lethal Weapon'

Much of my early childhood is a blank and the only early memory I have is of waking up in a dormitory-type room in a bed covered by a bright red blanket. Maybe it was a hospital ward or maybe a nursery.

Our mother Jessica, known as Jessie, was born into a large family. There were four brothers, Bobby, Alfie, Johnny and Arthur, and four sisters, Rose, Becky, Mary and our mother who is the youngest sister. Our grandparents were Rebecca and Alfred Marsh. Alfred Marsh was a hard-drinking, fighting man who commanded a lot of respect in our district. Eighty or 90 years ago he started a sawdust contracting business at 417 Hackney Road, Bethnal Green. Briefly, how it worked was this. Our Grandad would go to various sawmills, collect the sawdust and put it into sacks. Then he would take it back to his small factory where it would be sifted, graded and re-sacked into the many different types of sawdust required for various forms of industry. For example, furriers would use certain types for cleaning furs, fishmongers another type and so on.

The profits were big so the competition was fierce and a lot of heads got busted in order to supply the dust to the customers.

When our Grandad first started, all the transporting was done by a costermonger's handbarrow but he rose to the top of the heap by buying a horse and cart. Later on, three of my uncles, Alfie, Bobby and Arthur, joined him at the factory and the firm became Marsh Bros Sawdust Contractors. When the firm got bigger the horse and cart was replaced by large lorries. Our Uncle Bobby bought a house at Walthamstow where he lived with his wife Lottie, son Derek and daughter Jean. Uncle Alfie bought a large house in Chingford. There is no recollection of him ever getting married, but he was a bit of a ladies' man. Our Uncle Arthur lived on the second and third floor of the factory in Hackney Road with his wife Minnie and five sons, Tommy, Bobby, Arthur, Johnny and Steve. It was a large building and the machinery for packing and weighing the sawdust was kept in the basement. The ground floor was the office and storage place. Later on in the mid-Seventies I was to take this building over and turn it into an illegal drinking club and spieler, with a car sales forecourt and shop premises acting as a front.

My Aunt Rose, Uncle Chris and their children, Chris and his sister Patsy, lived in Hoxton where they ran two stalls in the market selling fruit and veg. Aunt Mary and her husband George and their two children, Joan and Barbara, moved out to Hounslow. Our Gran finished up living in an old bug-infested block of flats near the Elephant and Castle in South London. Aunt Becky lived in the same block of flats with her son John. Our Uncle John lived with his wife Eadie in Hoxton.

In my family there were just the three of us – my mother, my brother Ron and me. Ron was a talented artist and although we lived in a violent world he could paint serene and peaceful pictures. Most of them are seascapes, landscapes and beautiful oriental scenes done in pastel shades. He painted some pictures with a doctor's syringe to convey a certain effect. This was his own idea. I remember when we were kids and when we were growing up he would often tell me about a different beautiful world that he could see in his mind's eye. It was full of colours unseen in our present world. He described this new world he saw as going beyond space. It always surprised me that he could see so much beauty in spite of the brutal world we live in. He fervently believed in all he spoke of, and in this way he was unique.

We never knew our father, as he left us when we were very young. Our mother never received any maintenance or state handouts so times were pretty hard. But what we lacked in the way of material things and fine foods we made up for with a caring and unselfish love. All in all, things must have been extremely difficult for a woman on her own to clothe and feed two young children, specially when you think there was a war on. We moved about quite a lot, finally settling in Princess May Road, Dalston, where my brother Ron and I attended Princess May Junior School.

After our father had left us, our mother took us to live in a house in Tottenham owned by a man called Joe Ferrari. I don't remember much about him as he was in the army and away most of the time. He had a son who was also called Ron but he wasn't around because he was in the army too. In Tottenham my brother Ron and I both attended Rowland Hill School. This was in the middle of World War Two and air raids were quite frequent. During the raids the three of us would sleep under the stairs of the house. On one occasion we did take some bedding to the local underground station but it was so crowded with people and so noisy with children crying that we never went back.

I found the Blitz exciting, especially when I saw the flying-bombs – the Doodlebugs – with their familiar drone and smoke and flame coming from the rear. When I knew one was going to drop I would head in that direction and see a building on fire or smashed to smithereens, but the ARP – air raid wardens – would always shoo us away from the debris where I would be frantically searching for shrapnel. I began to loathe the ARP, who thrived on their little bit of power, especially of an evening when they would patrol the streets shouting, 'Put that light out!'

Two of the boys I went to school with lost arms in the bombing and I saw many corpses unearthed from the ruins and taken away on a stretcher covered up with a blanket. One day I found a large piece of shrapnel with blood on it and a blue beret with a jagged tear also smothered in blood. We really ran wild in those days –

perhaps things would have been different if we had a father. Throughout the war we rarely went short of the basic needs and were a lot better fed than many other children. To help out, Ron and I shoplifted when and where we could.

When I had just turned 11 a friend said he was going to be evacuated into the country where he would be riding horses and living on a farm with all kinds of animals. It sounded so exciting that I convinced my mother to get me evacuated. I suppose because she had my well-being at heart and thought I would be well looked after in the country and eating proper food instead of some of the make-do wartime rations of dried eggs, whale meat sausages and carrot marmalade that we got in London, she agreed to let me go.

I remember my mother packing my suitcase and making me some sandwiches for the journey. She tied an identification label around my neck and took me to join a group of other schoolchildren. I never knew where I was going and neither did she. Hour after hour I was on the train until I reached my destination. It finally dawned on me that I was miles from home and I wondered if I would ever see my mother and Ron again. I realised I had made a mistake in leaving them in bomb-torn London and felt selfish and guilty. I was also worried that Ron would think I was a coward and only worried about my own safety.

When we got off the train we were all taken into a large reception hall. I think I was there for about two days. People would come in and look us children over and I noticed that all the clean, polite and neatly dressed ones seemed to get picked, and all the raggedly dressed ones like me were ignored until the pick of the consignment had gone. I thought if I played up enough and became indifferent I would be sent back to London. But finally I was picked and whisked off to a house in a village that turned out to be Darwen in Lancashire. The people were kind to me. I never went to school during the two weeks I was there and spent my days in the long grass catching grass snakes. All this was new to me.

As soon as I was installed in the house they asked me a lot of questions, like where I came from and so on. I made out I couldn't understand their dialect and kept saying, 'What? What?' I also started using bad language in the hope that they would send me back to London. I knew Ron wouldn't let me down so I wrote to him saying I was making plans to get home. I told him where I was and asked him to arrange to get someone up here as I couldn't understand a word these people were saying and I'm sure they were Chinese or something.

Within two weeks I was sent home to resume my private war with the air raid wardens. I saw them as oppressors and in my young mind Hitler was someone else who hated the ARP as much as I did. I never knew what the war was about and was content causing havoc for everyone who gave me any grief.

The manager of the local cinema was one of our enemies because he tried to bar us for bunking in (getting in without paying), so spasmodically Ron and I and our friends would go to the cinema armed with glass bottles. We would sit in the back row waiting till everyone was engrossed in watching a love scene, then we would roll the bottles on the floor. They would start their descent down the slope, colliding into the iron legs of the seats. In a couple of minutes the cinema would be in uproar with all the lights going on and the manager and his staff heading straight for us. We thought it was hilarious and couldn't stop laughing and he knew it was us but couldn't prove it. He raised his hand as if to strike one of us and we said in unison, 'Just you fucking try it!' He could see he'd met his match in us and left us alone.

Although we had this close bond, Ron and I had our arguments and fights with one another. Sometimes these fights would last for ages, but neither of us would quit until we were both burnt out. Nobody would interfere with us when we were fighting for fear we would turn on them, which we did on a couple of occasions. We considered our fights a personal thing. The fights were only with our fists. We never went to the extreme of using a weapon or gouging eyes like we would in dirty streetfighting.

We didn't take much notice of the war, for we were more concerned with our own private wars with other gangs of kids in the area. Young children and puny children were quite safe from us. We preferred to fight bigger and older kids as the victory was more of an achievement. To us, fighting was a way of life but Ron and I had the edge over the opposition as we had the ability to co-operate as a team. Although our world revolved around each other we had other friends and a lot of fun.

Ron and I were seldom at home in the daytime. Much of our time was spent over at the local open-air swimming baths in the summer months or playing amongst the rubble of bombed-out buildings in our search for shrapnel. Our mother used to work as a riveter at Harris Lebuses at Tottenham Hale where she helped make invasion barges. Things were very scarce so we helped as best we could by going out with a Guy for a few days around 5 November or making a grotto with leaves, pebbles, sticks and anything else we could put our hands on.

Then, when I was about 11, I and a friend called Teddy Leyton did our first scam. We would get a shoebox, put some old broken crockery in it and wrap it up in brown paper, or fancy paper if we could get it, so that it looked like a present. Then we'd bunk on to the underground to Piccadilly, purposefully bump into a Yank (preferably an officer) and drop the parcel. Then Teddy and I would pretend to cry and soon a crowd would gather. Teddy would be inconsolable and would rattle the parcel so that all the breakages could be heard. I would cry some more and explain that we had come all the way from North London to buy Teddy's mother a small tea set for a present and the American had bumped into him and knocked it to the ground. Sometimes the crowd would get quite hostile towards the Yank, but I would intervene on his behalf saying it was only an accident. For this he was usually grateful and he'd give us a pound. More often than not some of the onlookers would put a bit of silver in our hand, and this plus the pound from the Yank would sometimes add up to two pounds.

My years in school I can remember quite vividly. I was always in scraps and my mother was constantly being summoned to see the headmaster. One of the incidents was because I had assaulted a teacher. I was aged about 12 at the time and a teacher had publicly humiliated me by standing me on a chair in front of the entire class and shaping up to me, taunting me by saying, 'Come on Webby, you're as big as me now.' I was so angry at this humiliation that I got off the chair, clenched my fists and at the precise moment when he was in range I kicked him in the balls, then punched him in the face with all my might. I am not proud of this but I think on his part it was most tactless and I just couldn't let it go. My mother was called to the school, which was nothing new. I explained to her that I was provoked so she was aware of the situation and at the meeting she said her piece. There was no point in suspending me as I was an habitual truant anyway. The headmaster told my mother that he was aware of some of the beatings other boys had suffered at Ron's and my hands, that we excelled in intimidating others and that I was a born leader and hard to cope with because of that. I certainly knew that if people were frightened of you there was nothing you could not get. Even as a schoolboy I realised that people's fear and ignorance gives you access to them and this lesson stayed with me throughout my life.

In those days the use of the school cane after school hours was the norm. I was the most rebellious and therefore the most caned boy in the school. Normally the punishment was six canings so you held your hand out and received three lashings on each hand. Normally the teacher would aim to hit your fingertips where it hurt most. What with that and the bombing and all the villainy going on around me, these were the contributing factors that played a great part in forming my outlook on life. From an early age Ron and I took the role of being the men of the family, for having no father we saw ourselves as the protectors of our mum.

Ron and I were very popular with the children we hung around with, although we were always getting into fights. Maybe this was because we had no father for guidance so we got out of hand. A lot of the fighting we got involved in was not of our doing but because the other kids found out we had been put down at the school as 'Ferrari', which was an Italian name. This was not our real surname but the man my mother was living with was called Ferrari. So the other kids began taunting us by calling us 'Hi-Ti's', which was their slang for 'Italians'. At first we did not realise their meaning because we had always been just Billy and Ron – we never even knew our surname was really Webb.

19

It was an insult to be called Italian when the country was at war with Italy, so we had to take drastic action to put this little gang of loudmouths in their place. We had quite a reputation and the only way we knew how to keep it was with brute force. Of course we had our own little gang of toughs, but this 'Hi-Ti' business was a personal affront to us and so it could only be settled by us. My brother and I made our battle plans. I was really excited about it all, as now the time had arrived when I could use a lethal weapon for the first time in my life. I had the good fortune to have had a weapon made up for me sometime before, and now I had an opportunity to use it on a human target. And who better than a boy I'd never got on with? As he was also the head of the local gang and a bully, he needed to be hurt badly.

Several weeks prior to these 'Hi-Ti' taunts, I had got hold of several big steel nuts. I got a man who worked in a small welding factory to file down the threads inside the nuts and weld them together to make a knuckleduster. I gave him a rough diagram of what I wanted and he completed it in his dinner hour. He was too dim to realise that he could get into big trouble legally, so I told him that the implement he was making was to replace a part that had broken on my cousin's swing. I managed to get five Park Drive cigarettes for him and that way I acquired my first made-to-order piece of armoury. I could not wait to try it out, so on the way home I slipped it on my hand and punched a wooden boarded-up door. I was over the moon when I saw the deep impressions I had made on the wood. The only problem was that the impact gave me a bit of a jolt, but I overcame this by putting some material in my fist to cushion the blow. Then I found that no matter how hard I punched, the padding stopped the jolt and any pain.

We decided to sort out this kid and his gang the following day. After considering various plans of attack we decided to do the business in a confined space where they could not escape. We got to school early that morning and hid half a cricket stump in the boys' toilet in case we had the need for it. Normally any fights took place in the school playground but these did not go unnoticed and were normally broken up by a school-teacher.

Finally dinnertime came and my brother and I kept the boys' toilets under surveillance. When the big loud-mouthed boy and four of his friends made their way into the toilets to have a smoke, I put a pair of woollen gloves on, slipped on the knuckleduster and pulled a woollen mitten over the knuckleduster in order to conceal it. Then I walked through the entrance of the toilet, straight up to the loud-mouthed boy and smashed him in the face. He dropped like a sack. Then I spun round and tore into another boy; gave him a right-hander and kicked his arse to help him on his way. My Ron was at the other door with the cricket stump belting whoever tried to escape our wrath. As I punched the loud-mouth I could see his face more or less explode wide open and such was the power of the weapon that he soon hit the deck. Within a minute it was all over and no one had retaliated with even a punch.

So that I would not be caught with a lethal weapon, I had a pre-arranged plan to hand the knuckleduster to a friend who was close by so that he could take it home. This is a method I have used ever since. In due course Ron and I were called in front of the headmaster. I claimed I was not the aggressor, that I merely defended myself, that the boy had slipped over and the damage was caused by him hitting the water pipes and fittings. None of his friends wanted to get involved in case of repercussions. Fortunately no one knew about the use of the knuckleduster.

When the war ended Joe Ferrari came home from the army. It was then that I realised I had inherited a father I never knew existed, for until then I had never been aware that our mother was living with Ferrari as man and wife. I don't know if Ron knew the situation but as far as we were concerned nothing had changed. The only thing of some confusion was that we had also acquired a brother, or I should say a step-brother, also named Ron, who had also been demobbed from the army. I was a bit indifferent to this new family member. I can remember him sauntering about the house bare-chested with a long-bladed knife in his waistband. He was in his twenties but he was still very wary of us even though we were only schoolboys. I remember he often tried his hardest to make trouble between my brother and me but the trust and bond we had with each other was too strong. This he could not comprehend.

Just before I was 14 years old our mother called me and Ron into the kitchen and told us to pay attention to what she had to say. She went on to tell us that she had located our real father as she wanted a divorce from him. She had discovered that after he had left us he had married another woman bigamously. We never really understood any of it as we had never even heard the word bigamy before, let alone what it meant. Later our mother told us she would have to go to court where our father was to be tried for bigamy. I believe the court she mentioned was the Old Bailey. I don't know what went on at the court but I do know that he never went to prison although he should have. After our mother got her divorce, Joe Ferrari was anxious to marry her, but she was not keen, so for almost a year the three of us moved in with our Uncle Arthur at the sawdust factory in Bethnal Green. We lived there with our aunt and uncle and our five cousins.

Our mum used to spend the day with her sister, Rose, and we would gamble our pennies up the wall or play cards for small stakes. We knew our aunt's street as Essex Street but because of its notoriety after a policeman was murdered there, it was re-named Shenfield Street. The police were most reluctant to enter Essex Street by themselves even though they knew it was a haven of thieves and fences and that there were warrants out for many of the residents.

Our Uncle Bob and Uncle Alfie were still running the sawdust business at Hackney Road but we never saw much of them as they finished early and went back to their homes in Walthamstow and Chingford. I never went to school whilst we were living in Bethnal Green. I don't know what Ron was doing but he was getting money somewhere, so I never went short. I was really happy in Hackney as our cousins were good company and ran wild like Ron and me.

Then we moved back to Tottenham. We learned that Joe Ferrari and his son Ron were emigrating to Australia. Maybe this was the reason we moved back to the East End. Our mother obviously had her reasons. I think it's a bit late in the day to ask her now. She had always done what she considered best for Ron and me and made many sacrifices. All she ever seemed to do was work and worry about us. She gave us endless lectures but I think she realised that we never absorbed anything she tried to press home as always within days we were back in trouble and more complaints were laid on our doorstep. But all through those days she never once raised her hand to us.

CHAPTER TWO

I Learn about Protection

When I reached the age of 14 I left school officially. I had no qualifications whatsoever so I went along to the Labour Exchange (now called the Job Centre) and told them I wanted a job. They gave me an introduction to a local furniture factory so I went along and arranged to start on the Monday next at 8 a.m. When the Monday came I arrived about ten minutes late, so already I'd set off on the wrong foot. The first day seemed like an eternity, and to make it worse I had no overalls. I was supposed to sweep the floors and clear up after everyone else, just a general help at everyone's beck and call. All my clothes were dusty and they tried to make a dogsbody of me, which I found really humiliating and degrading.

When I arrived for work the following day I pulled the foreman and told him I wanted to finish up so could I have my day's money. He informed me that I would have to give a week's notice. I told him that I did not understand all this talk about a week's notice as this was my first job. Fortunately he was a decent sort of man and took pains to explain the situation. He told me to just see the week out and make myself scarce. So I hid myself in the open yard at the rear of the factory where I would sit for most of the working hours. I also made sure I had long dinner breaks.

During one of my lunchtime breaks, which was spent outside the factory, I became good friends with a boy named Tommy Etherington who was about the same age as me. Like me he was keen on boxing and belonged to the Enterprise Boxing Club. Sadly Tommy died of cancer a few years ago. His sister Doris was married to Tommy Welsh, otherwise known as The Bear, who became a Kray minder and was the only one of the Kray firm I stayed good friends with. The Bear was to cross paths with me often over the years. He was a giant of a man, a good six foot three and weighing 18 stone, so no one took liberties with him. He had done a lot of professional boxing and had sparred with Tommy Farr, who was the British heavyweight champion in the 1930s. The Bear was a likeable man with a kind face who also had a humorous side. One evening he walked into a pub and when the pianist saw him he started playing *The Teddy Bear's Picnic*, which The Bear thought was in bad taste. He walked to the piano and said, 'I like that tune', and stood over the man until he had played it 12 times. He had known the Krays since they were boys and stood in the dock with them at their trial in 1969 where he got three years for ABH (actual bodily harm).

The Bear's striking blonde wife, Doris, had a clairvoyant power and whenever I visited her and her sister Sheila in later years I always felt that she was reading my mind. I believe all this family were clairvoyant because I would also get this strange feeling when I was in Tommy Etherington's company.

Shortly after I had walked out on my first job that I found so unpleasant, my brother Ron got me a job with him for a firm of builders called Quigley and Murphy who were a couple of Irishmen with a really good sense of humour. They seemed to spend most of their time playing cards in the office where I would occasionally join them and have a few hands. Joe Quigley was an ex-boxer who would love to spar with me in the small yard where various pieces of building plant were kept. Joe Quigley taught me a lot about boxing, especially all the dirty tricks in what he called the noble art.

Nobody seemed to do much work and I believe most of the

work, if not all, was on a time and material basis, so they did not seem to mind how long a contract took. I imagine they must have had good contacts in some government office somewhere. There was no foreman as such, so Ron and I would come and go as we pleased. More often than not we never bothered to turn up for a couple of days at a time and nothing was ever said. This freedom allowed us to move around and meet quite a few people who could be assets to us later, although at that time we had no definite plans.

When I was doing this job I don't really recall having any inkling or sense of direction and never knew what fate had tricked out for me. But my future was shaped by an elderly man called Bob who originally came from Portsmouth and who owned a local snooker hall called the Lancaster Snooker Club. Meeting Bob was to change my life and it helped to shape my future. Until then I had never been inside a snooker club and I found myself really fascinated at the atmosphere of this smoke-filled place. From then on I believe I knew what fate had in store for me.

Bob was a really likeable man, but some of the local yobs were taking liberties in his club, like not paying for their tables and sometimes causing other trouble. Being a stranger in our area, Bob had no friends and he asked Ron and me if we would help sort out his problems. Ron and I told him we would. We were new to this kind of business, but we knew you had to do things right. So that night we got tooled up with bayonets, which were very easy to come by at that time, and went to the club. Then we sat at the bar talking to the owner whilst waiting for the yobs to show their faces.

We were told they normally arrived at the club at about 10 p.m., after they had a drink in a pub. Prior to them arriving we had told Bob the owner that it was best we did the business outside as there would probably be a lot of blood shed, which might splatter on to his snooker tables and ruin them, or furniture might be unavoidably smashed. We waited until about 2 a.m. but they gave it a miss that night, so we arranged to return the following night. It was just gone 10 p.m. when they arrived. There were five of them in all, and the owner rushed over to me and told me that one of the five had never been in the club before. I pulled that one aside and told him to fuck off as his mates were going to get hurt really bad. After he had gone we told the others to step outside as we wanted to talk to them. As soon as they were outside the club we attacked them and beat them senseless. For good measure we smashed their American car to pieces. They never came near the club again. I never have had any time for liberty-takers who prey on vulnerable old people. I suppose that although Ron and I only did this as a favour to an old guy it was our first taste of providing protection. Everything stemmed from that club and although I was only 17 at the time I soon knew all the basic rules on protection and whom to approach and how.

After that we spent a lot of time in the club which was open until 6 or 7 a.m. and we organised poker schools and crap games there. The old guy was pleased with us. There was hardly any trouble and his takings rocketed. He still worked behind the bar serving drinks, and he could afford to give us a good rake off for keeping the place peaceful. Although this was on a friendly basis and the old chap really needed our help, when word got around of what we'd done to the liberty-takers no one else started any trouble. This is what I call real protection, for the old guy really needed us to save his business. If we hadn't he would have been ruined.

Around this time I used to occasionally frequent a restaurant in Green Lanes, Harringay. Whilst I was in there one day I was introduced to a well-spoken man who I learned was one of the ringmasters of Tom Arnold's Circus that performed for a couple of months each Christmas at Harringay Arena. This man was the one who hired people for the circus. He went on talking to me and dropping hints so I told him to get to the point, whatever it was. He then said he was supposed to hire a certain amount of staff but he could run the show with a reduced staff. If he hired me, I had to turn up on the day they hired the casual staff and my name would be put on the payroll. Then all I had to do was collect and sign for my wages each week and I would have half of the money which was £9. I had to give him the other half. I never ever saw this man sober and I later learned that he was an alcoholic.

Half of £9 was quite a lot of money for me at a time when a packet of cigarettes cost about 1/6d (seven and a half pence) and a pint of beer cost about a shilling (five pence) but I thought I deserved the lion's share. So we agreed that I took £5 and he had £4. I then said, 'What about Ron?' I knew he couldn't really say no, so the same arrangements were made and everyone was happy, especially us as we had never done a day's work for anywhere near as much as a fiver.

One Saturday after I had signed the wages book I told Ron I wanted to stay and watch the show as I had never seen a circus before. I found myself a good seat and watched the various acts. Above all I wanted to see the lions, the so-called Kings of the Jungle, but what I saw fell a long way short of what I had anticipated. Instead of seeing magnificent creatures in all their glory, I saw only cowering creatures robbed of all their dignity and completely broken in spirit. It made me feel quite sad.

Afterwards I decided to go to one of the bars for a drink. After I had been there a couple of minutes I noticed a pretty young showgirl. She was in her circus costume, which was like a ringmaster, but instead of trousers she had black fishnet tights, high-heeled shoes, a sequined tail-coat and a top hat. Up until that moment I had never felt the need to go to all the bother of making myself known to any girl, but this girl was really something else and I really wanted to get to know her. I noticed she was aware of me but I decided that discretion was the better part of valour, so I finished my drink, left the bar and made a point of nodding to her and saying, 'Goodnight'. So at least I wasn't a complete stranger to her.

The following Tuesday I went to the circus bar again at the same time and she arrived about ten minutes later. I nodded in recognition but all I could think of saying was, 'I like the outfit', meaning her ringmaster's costume. Her name was Josephine and I found myself confronted by everything that was feminine. At first she probably thought I was older than 17. I spent the best part of the evening with her apart from the times she left me in the bar whilst she changed into various costumes to do her stuff. I asked her to go out with me and we arranged to meet the following

Sunday in a Greek restaurant opposite the Harringay Arena.

The owners of this restaurant knew both Ron and me as we often went in with two or three friends. A few years later we began to draw protection money from this and other restaurants and establishments in the area, as it had become hugely populated by the Irish communities, some of whom could be troublesome in drink and cause a lot of havoc. But at this time the restaurant was trouble-free.

Josephine was the first romance of my life. Even though I was 17 I was still a virgin. I had never really taken much notice of girls up until now, as mine had been very much a man's world and I was mixing with and accepted by adult people. Of course I knew a few old slappers who would more than likely oblige me, but this girl was not just attractive, she was very intelligent and cultured. I got a straight friend to drive me to the restaurant for the date and told him not to open his mouth as he might say something detrimental about me or my lifestyle. For a couple of weeks I saw a lot of Josephine and then the circus moved on and I lost touch with her for a while.

Ron and I were doing pretty well. We were still working officially with Quigley and Murphy for a few hours a week and had our name on Tom Arnold's payroll as well. So we were not short of money. I have always dressed pretty sharp and in those days had my suits made by Frank Wood who had his tailor shop on the Kingspond Road, Dalston. In later years I learned the Kray twins also had their suits made there.

One day when I had been with Josephine I was late for a date I had with Ron. When I got there Ron was a bit annoyed as we had arranged to meet a couple of guys at Stamford Hill which I had forgotten about. We drove to the E & A Salt Beef Restaurant at Stamford Hill. When we arrived the two guys were still waiting. Apparently what had happened was that one of these fellers, Vic, had got into an argument with a family called Dulligan who had a bit of a reputation in South Tottenham at that time. I was on good terms with the Dulligans and they owed me a favour. A couple of weeks previously when I was at their house visiting Jean Dulligan, a girl of about 17, I had been asked to eject her father, Jacko

Dulligan, from the house, which I did. He had been coming home drunk and causing havoc and threatening the family. I knew Jacko could be a pest. On one occasion he made a defamatory remark about a good friend of mine and so I gave him a terrible beating. It was so bad he was terrified of me and would go to great lengths to avoid me. When I got to the house he was sitting in an armchair. I just said, 'Come on, pack your things, you're out.' He remembered the beating he took from me and within a few minutes he had gone and left his door key with his wife. Shortly after that she got an injunction to keep him away from the house.

Anyhow, Ron asked me to intervene on behalf of these guys to try to patch it up. I didn't really want to get involved as I never knew them, but because Ron wanted it done I never questioned his reasoning. The following evening I went to the Dulligans' house. Mrs Dulligan answered the door and invited me in. Both the Dulligan brothers, Pat and Johnny, were at home and I asked what the problem was with this feller called Vic. Johnny Dulligan told me that Vic had been drinking in The Eagle pub in Tottenham High Road a couple of weeks ago and had been abusive to Johnny Dulligan who gave him a beating and that the fella called Vic was just trying to get other people involved to sort his problems out and fight his battles. When I told Ron the situation we gave Vic and his friend a beating for trying to get us involved. Over the years we got a lot of this from people. I think Ron was too sympathetic, never really realising that if someone got hurt badly and went to the police we would be the ones in the dock as we were getting well known.

By this time we had stopped working for Quigley and Murphy but remained on good terms with them. I used to drop into their office often and have a few games of poker and when the weather was good Joe Quigley would still like to spar with me in the yard. I was doing a lot of boxing then at the Langham Boxing Club but I think I learnt more from him than I did at the club. By this time most of our spare time was spent looking after the Lancaster Snooker Club and making sure it was running nice and clean.

Ron and I never spent much time at home. Our mother had got remarried to John Gage, who was a street bookie's runner and collected bets in various streets in Hoxton but could mostly be found in Hoxton Square. This was before betting offices were legalised and the only way a punter could get a bet on without going racing was to place the bet with a street bookie's runner. John Gage was nicknamed 'Speedy' by the locals as he was a bit rapid in making his departure when the Old Bill had a purge on. He got nicked a few times but these only amounted to fines which were paid by the bookmakers he worked for. Half the time he used to pocket the no-hoper bets. He liked a drink and a bet but he thought a lot of our mother and left us to our vices, so we got along with no interference.

All in all we were doing well. We slept late, as most nights we would be in the snooker hall or socialising with friends and acquaintances at an all-night cafe at Stamford Hill opposite the E & A Salt Beef Bar. Much of the clientèle there were Jewish businessmen and cab drivers. Tony Mulla would frequently be there. He was a big German-Greek maniac who got into mad rages and cried a lot. He was always looking for an easy mark and even swindled his own relations. He was connected by marriage to the two Italian brothers known as Shelley and Pepi who owned a restaurant in Tottenham. Before betting off the track was legalised Shelley and Pepi made an illegal book and were bookmakers in a small way. When Mulla heard about this he started phoning in bets knowing they would not refuse him. He finished up running up a big bill which he never intended to pay. Later he went into owning pornographic shops in Soho, which led to his violent death. I never liked Mulla and always thought of him as a liberty-taker. If our eyes ever met in the cafe he would grudgingly nod in recognition but we never ever spoke.

Anyhow, Tony Mulla heard that a fella called Arthur Risley had quite a bit of money tucked away and he used to frighten him into drawing various amounts out to give to him until it was all dried up, or maybe Arthur got wise and put it in another account. Mulla was a real bully who took what he could when he could. He had no principles whatsoever.

This Arthur Risley was one of two brothers who used to spend some time in the Stamford Hill salt beef bar. Arthur's brother was called Billy and they were known as the 'Sus brothers' as they were always being arrested and charged with being 'suspected persons'. The 'sus law' enabled the police to arrest any person whom they knew had a criminal record and to swear in court that the man was acting suspiciously. It was an automatic conviction as you couldn't very well challenge police evidence. The law has now been repealed, but whilst it was in force it gave a police officer absolute authority over any convicted felon. Believe me, prisons were full of known criminals serving three-month sentences for being a 'suspected person'. I can assure you that no evidence was required other than a police officer standing up in court and saying he saw a known felon acting suspiciously – that was all that was needed to get a conviction. It never seemed to enter a magistrate's head that the same Old Bill (mostly CID) were in front of the same magistrate week after week with the same old spiel. When this law was in force I knew happily married men reluctant to return home after their prison sentences for fear of being nicked on a trumped-up charge.

When Tom Arnold's circus came back to Harringay Arena I was anxious to meet Josephine again because she had made a lasting impression on me so I went to see her. My Uncle Arthur had been giving me a couple of driving lessons and a friend had lent me his car for a couple of days so I arrived smartly dressed with a decent car outside. I never bothered to see any of the acts, stationed myself at the bar and waited hopefully for Josephine. After a while she made an appearance. She was really classy and seemed a cut above the normal run of girls but I suppose the glamorous costume and painstaking make-up set her apart. Nevertheless, I was pleased that she was glad to see me. I think by this time she knew I was not kosher and was free with my money.

I was always respectful to her and curbed any bad language. I never told her about my way of life, for even though she was intelligent, it was unlikely she would understand. I didn't like to lie to her so when she asked me what I did for a living I told her I had a bit of say in a gambling club. I did not consider that this was an outright lie as I did have a say in who stayed and who went in the snooker club I was still minding. I'm sure now that I loved her at that time more than I loved any other girl.

If I was not in love with Josephine, I must have been really besotted and infatuated. But I always felt that any long-lasting love affair would be doomed as one day she would find out what I was all about. Sometimes when I was with her I would meet acquaintances. Anyone could see they were out and out villains even though I was careful and selective about where I took her. I was a teenager and teenagers are expected to do wild things, yet somehow when I was with her I was filled with a feeling of guilt about what I was and always unable to tell her what I was at. Probably the worst of it was that she never questioned me and this robbed me of any chance of showing that I was still capable of honour.

CHAPTER THREE

I Meet the Krays

In 1949, Ron and I started to go to The Royal dance hall, Tottenham. Though we never bothered to learn to dance, it was a nice plush place where we could meet friends, old and new, and socialise. We liked to go there as it was a pleasant atmosphere and ideal for planning the future and relaxing. It was open in the afternoon and evening, but we preferred the afternoons when it was less busy.

We had acquired a large following by then and to assert our superiority we had many battles with the opposition. These fights usually involved lethal weapons like flick knives, coshes, chains and all the rest. One lot in The Royal called themselves the Corner Boys because the corner part of the dance hall where they sat was the more spacious, with soft furnishings and tables, and the most comfortable. That was their corner and everyone else had to keep out of it. The Corner Boys were straight working men, some in their thirties, who thought that because they had been frequenting The Royal for a number of years they had the right to the more luxurious surroundings. After we got shot of them we were the superior ones and we dominated the corner.

We always knew when any new mob appeared at The Royal.

One week a gang of five or six came to our attention. Soon after they appeared a couple of girls had their purses stolen from their handbags and the empty purses were found later in the gents' toilets. After that we kept this new mob under scrutiny and left one of our gang to watch near the vicinity of the toilets. Later Tommy Etherington and I were beckoned over and told that three of the new gang were in one of the gents' cubicles. We stormed in and kicked open the cubicle door to find them there with the purses. We lost no time in dragging them out by the scruffs of their necks and beating them till they begged for mercy. We took the purses and all the money they had on them and told them to get out of The Royal and never come back. We gave the purses back to the girls, plus what money was theirs, and kept the surplus ourselves. You may think this was no concern of mine, but I think it was a despicable thing to rob a working girl of her hard-earned wages. Other fights in The Royal occurred when people would try to oust us but they were never successful.

The staff of The Royal showed us a lot of respect, especially Bill the Bouncer. He had a bald head and a broken nose. He never interfered but just let us get on with it. This was because he took care not to inflame any of our large mob, as many of them would be armed with lethal weapons of their liking and were known to use them without a second's hesitation. So Bill the Bouncer knew that if anything started it would be a total war which he had no chance of controlling – we were a bunch of streetwise kids who had all been brought up in the violent world of war-torn London. Our playgrounds had been bomb-sites and our most prized possessions were pieces of shrapnel from bombs.

Soon after we took over the corner the Kray twins started to frequent The Royal. We had heard of them, and they had heard of us – news travels fast by word of mouth. Sometimes as a show of force they would arrive with their mob in the back of an army lorry driven by a friend called Googie Lane, an army man. He was, I believe, in the RASC and stationed at Regent's Park Barracks, London. I suppose there must have been near enough 20 in this Kray gang. We got to know some of them pretty well and we got on all right with most of them. Many of them got to be well known in later years. One was Ronnie Knight who later married Barbara Windsor, the actress. He now lives in Spain. Another was Kenny Lynch, the coloured comedian and singer often seen on TV.

We became aware of the Kray twins soon after their first appearance in the dance hall. At first I never paid them a lot of attention and thought of them as a couple of actors out to impress people – all night long they sat poker-faced glaring at everyone. They had their own little gang always close at hand, which proved that they didn't then, and never would, have the courage to have a fight on their own. This proved to be the case throughout their reign.

After the Krays had been frequenting The Royal for a couple of weeks we heard that they had recently been nicked with members of their gang for beating a young kid senseless, and they were going around gloating about this conquest. It was a boy of 16 called Harvey. He had been beaten around the eyes and face with a bicycle chain and well kicked. The twins were named by witnesses and arrested. The magistrate said they were 'animals' and should be taught a lesson. He sent them to the Old Bailey for trial. It came out that the witnesses were warned off, one girl being told she would be razored if she talked. Harvey himself, who was still in hospital, was warned not to give evidence and the twins were acquitted. The case was reported in the local paper and the Krays were so proud of this that they carried the article around in their pockets to show to their friends.

Shortly after this the twins were put on probation for causing bodily harm to a police constable outside Pellici's Cafe in Bethnal Green Road. They had been told to move along because they were causing obstruction and Ronnie punched him in the face in front of a dozen witnesses. This time they were put on probation after the magistrate described the attack as 'cowardly'.

As the undisputed rulers of The Royal we realised that the Krays might cause us a problem. Their cousin, Rita, used to go to the dance hall. She was a real stuck-up little bitch and always generated a lot of trouble. One evening a friend of mine came over to my table and told me the Krays were coming over on the Saturday with their little firm to sort him out as he had insulted a girl who, unbeknown to him, turned out to be their cousin Rita. He had asked her for a dance and because she refused he had said, 'What are you, a fucking princess?' I told him not to worry as I would see my brother Ron and arrange to have some of our friends come along. At the time I was pleased about the incident as for some time there had been a kind of cold war going on with the Krays. Often I would catch one of them staring. I can't remember ever seeing them smile, they were always wooden-faced and surrounded by members of their gang.

We knew the Krays would turn up at The Royal in great numbers. So during the week we made our battle plans with great attention to detail. Many of our mob with weapons on their person were placed at strategic points, and other weapons hidden around the premises where they could be got at when needed. We knew that when the twins came they'd be with one of their closest friends, Patsy Aucott, so these three were to be our main targets. We also knew they'd be well armed so we selected the most ruthless and proven of our gang to stay alongside my brother and me and pit ourselves against the Krays themselves. Finally Saturday came and we arrived in force all tooled up for trouble. In our plans it was decided that I would tackle Ronnie Kray and have someone guarding my back as he would no doubt have a hand-picked man with him.

Gradually the customers started to drift into the dance hall. We knew most of the Krays' allies by sight and were not surprised to see two or three make an appearance and then disappear. I realised they were sent in as observers or spies to see what the opposition was. About half an hour later Reggie came in with about ten of his friends. His brother Ronnie was nowhere in sight. I noticed Reggie had his arm in plaster. He came straight over to me and said, 'I've got no argument with you.' I could see his cousin Rita in the background. He then said that someone who he believed was a friend of mine had insulted Rita. He said Rita wanted an apology from one of our gang and it didn't matter which one.

It seemed to me that he didn't want to fight. Perhaps it was because he had an arm in plaster, which seemed very convenient given the circumstances, or because his twin wasn't there – I always saw Ronnie as the evil instigator of bloodshed. We were ready to go into battle and we knew it would be a bloody one. But the outcome was that we could see that some sort of apology was in order and we decided to let it go. So I beckoned over the friend who was responsible and explained the situation. He then put matters right. Maybe the twins thought it was a moral victory of sorts but I know we both realised that if we had gone ahead both sides would have suffered enormous damage and wondered if it was really worth it on account of Rita's ideas about herself. On the other hand, perhaps they just didn't have the bottle to take us on when they saw our numbers.

This was our first confrontation with the twins but not the last. From that day on we just acknowledged each other by the occasional nod. No words were ever spoken. After that they never trod on our toes nor we on theirs. However, I was on friendly terms with some of their associates and members of their entourage, which peeved the Krays quite a bit.

When I first got to know the twins they were 'on the knocker' with their dad, Charlie Kray, and their Uncle Alf. The four of them would go out to various districts in London or in the suburbs and knock on street doors buying clothing in good condition, gold, silver, jewellery and the like. They would all meet at eight o'clock in the morning and drive off in an old car to any London suburb. Then all four of them would go off, each of them carrying a large empty sack. They would then all go their separate ways, knocking on doors and asking if the occupant had any clothing or small pieces of gold or silver to sell. All the gold and jewellery buying was done by Charlie Kray, their dad, or their Uncle Alf, as the twins had no idea about buying. Charlie and Alf had in their pockets a small set of scales for weighing gold and silver. The price they paid was a long way short of the real value, but they knew that if someone is hard-up enough they are easily tricked into parting with their goods. Reggie was a trier in this racket, but Ronnie wasn't so keen. When the others got back he would be sitting in the car saying he'd had no luck. Any old gold and silver in good condition was sold in the pub. The rest was sold as scrap. The overcoats were sold to a small shop in Middlesex Street, known as Petticoat Lane, and other items of clothing were sold by their Uncle Alf on a stall he ran in Cheshire Street market, Bethnal Green, and the Petticoat Lane Sunday market.

From the beginning I found Ronnie Kray to be what I considered over-sensitive about certain things. Later on he became really paranoid about the most trivial things so that many people gave him a lot of distance. No one, not even his twin, could talk to him without the risk of having his words distorted. I noticed that both of them were a bit hostile in their attitude to us and seemed to resent the repartee and familiarity we had with the manager of The Royal dance hall.

But the gang they built around them at the time were hardly a threat as I'm sure they were mostly schoolkids. They relied on numbers rather than quality. I think what infuriated the Krays was the complete disregard and total lack of interest we showed in them. My brother Ron thought it was humorous that night after night they appeared and just stood poker-faced and glaring. Not once did I see them dance or talk to girls. When my brother saw Ronnie Kray appear he would turn to me and laugh and say, 'I see Boot Nose is here again', meaning that Ronnie Kray has a slightly smaller version of a W. C. Fields nose.

It was about this time that I was first arrested. I was with Tommy Etherington on enclosed premises and we were charged with being there for unlawful purposes. For this I got six months as a young offender. Tommy was given a conditional discharge.

Josephine was back in town with Tom Arnold's circus and she made it clear she wanted to see more of me. One night when I had walked her home she suddenly kissed me full on the lips, then told me I could come any time I liked to see her. She was to be resting between bookings for a while and would have more time to spend with me. As soon as the show closed down I began to see her every day and took her to Cicero's restaurant in the West End, where my friend Billy Welsh's wife worked as a silver-service waitress, and to a few other selective places where I was known. By now Josephine knew my pedigree and even though she was so refined I believe she found it all a bit exciting. After a week or so she asked me if I would like to go to a small party at a friend's home as the parents would be away for the weekend.

The idea appealed to me so it was decided we would go together. When we arrived there were just three girls and two men. Someone put some slow music on and a couple started to dance. Josephine asked me to dance with her and I told her I didn't know how. Even though I spent so much time at The Royal and The Lyceum in the West End, I had not once been on the dance floor as to us those places, which were very plush, were just meeting places. She took me by the hand on to the floor. I felt like a fish out of water, but she helped me through a dance or two and eventually we sat down on a couch and talked together.

I had never given much thought as to her age and assumed she must have been around 18, and then she told me she was nearing 20. To put myself on a par with her I told her I was expecting my call-up papers any time and might be conscripted for two years. I was really infatuated with her and did not want her to feel I was too young for her, so I figured she would believe I was a young man, not a teenager. This made sense to me and I'm sure she got the drift of what I was saying and understood I wanted to keep hold of her. I was relieved when she said she had thought I was 20 or so, and acted as such. Soon the evening was coming to an end and I spent the night with her. This was my first love. I saw her every day for the next week or so. Ron got annoyed with me for spending so much time with her.

Then there was another period when she was on out-of-town bookings. The next time we met things had cooled down a bit between us and I had received my call-up papers. I realised there was no way I could handle a two-year duration in the army with some jumped-up little corporal ordering me around, so the future looked pretty bleak. I didn't suppose Josephine would relish the thought of having a fugitive from the army as a boyfriend, so I never bothered to express my views to her on what I considered an oppression and an injustice to my person, and I decided to forget all about her.

I have thought a lot about Josephine since those days. You must realise that at that period of my life there was nothing permanent about me. This led to great feelings of insecurity. I felt I could not offer her the security I so much wanted to give her. To compensate for this I was very free with my money, but at the same time given to fits of violent outbursts if she was ever attentive to someone else. Ashamedly, I found myself becoming jealous and disruptive and the cause of many unpleasant scenes. If fate had decided that we met a few years later I would have married her. Even though we were from different walks of life, we were compatible. But I doubt that she could have influenced me to have changed my lifestyle or my beliefs, as these were deeply rooted in me from an early age.

Next thing I was ordered to attend an army medical but before that date I was arrested with a friend of mine for being a suspected person and had my life sworn away by an over-zealous police officer. Due to the fact that I was soon to do my two years' national service I was let off with a hefty fine and bound over. The following week I was passed A1 for the army. I was interviewed by an officer and I told him I wanted no part of military service. If I had claimed to be a conscientious objector I would have been ordered to spend two years down a coal mine, but that seemed to me to be the worse of two evils.

CHAPTER FOUR

Thorns or Feathers

My call-up ruined any chance I had of pursuing my ambitions to become a successful boxer. When I first started at the Langham Boxing Club as a schoolboy, I was a bantamweight. Naturally, when I got older my weight increased and I had difficulty making lightweight division, so I fought as a light-welterweight. On a few occasions during our later stints of desertion I would frequent the Enterprise Boxing Club with the Krays. On more than one occasion I sparred with Reggie Kray and he could really punch. Apart from my spell as an amateur, I fought on many unlicensed shows. Sometimes the weight difference was as much as a stone either side, but most of the fights were rigged – just the same as it is today, at all levels, apart from amateur contests.

But my boxing ambitions were dashed in January 1951 when I was press-ganged into the army against my will. I arrived at Aldershot with other new recruits and was given an army uniform and had my hair shorn like a sheep. Each and every day I wandered around the barracks as I was not interested in joining in the classes or the childish army games. All the other recruits were alien to my way of life so I steered clear of them.

A week after I was called up for national service I had had

enough of getting up early in the mornings and spending my time with all these recruits who accepted everything that was flung at them. I hungered for life on the streets again and moving around with my kind of people. I preferred to keep myself to myself. But a guy from North London became friendly with me and told me about a bent doctor he knew in Hackney Road called Dr Feezie who would hand out certificates for two shillings and sixpence (12½ pence) a time. Each one would last for a week and all you needed to do was send the certificate off to your regiment and claim sick leave. I could not wait till the time came for me to get a weekend pass.

I got my first weekend pass on a Friday and on the Saturday morning I was one of the first patients at Dr Feezie's office. Several people were there already, but when the doctor came in and looked around he beckoned me in even though I was the last one into the waiting-room. He asked me what was the matter and, not knowing what to say, I told him I had constant stomach ache. Then without examining me he said, 'You've got gastric flu', and wrote a certificate to this effect saying I was unfit. He then asked me for two shillings and sixpence and gave me a certificate. When I joined Ron, who was waiting in the car, I told him how the doctor had ushered me into the surgery ahead of all the others. Ron replied, 'Well, he probably realised you was in the army and wanted a certificate, so he never saw you in the chair, all he saw was what resembled 2/6.' My visits to the surgery went on for several weeks. To my mind I had out-foxed the army and scored a minor victory. On one occasion I went to the doctor's only to find he was not on duty and the only person in the surgery was the charlady who promptly wrote me out a certificate. I was a bit shocked at this but soon it became common for after a short while I learned that the doctor had a drink problem.

This new-found freedom lasted for 13 weeks and I spent all my time with Ron visiting all our old haunts. Then I received a letter saying I was to go to Mill Hill in North London and undergo a medical examination by a military doctor. Of course I had no intention of going to Mill Hill or any other army establishment. During my 13 weeks' sick leave my regimental short haircut had grown. I decided the time had come for me to become a deserter. I think my first spell of being a deserter lasted about six weeks – I was new to it and a bit over-confident as to what and where I could go. I was soon captured, returned to my regiment and locked in the guardroom. The following day I appeared in front of the CO. I was as arrogant as ever but my CO must have overlooked this as he only sentenced me to 28 days' detention in the guardroom. He gave me the normal lecture that a man can make his bed with thorns or feathers but I had chosen to make mine with thorns. I knew he meant well, but he realised I was a lost cause. I suppose he was duty bound and had to try to reach me. He went on to say that hopefully the 28 days' detention he had awarded me had made me realise the folly of my ways. I find it a bit amusing when they say they are 'awarding' you a certain amount of days' detention. It's almost like they're bestowing a medal on you.

This was my first experience of detention and of the next three and a half years I spent in the army, most of it was as a deserter or in detention barracks. As for my army pay I saw nothing of that, for every time I deserted my so-called comrades would steal all my kit as soon as I was gone. The cost of this was deducted from my pay, but long before I was ever in credit I would desert again. I did make sure that every time I went on the run I took my greatcoat with me as there was a shop in the east end that was always good for 30 shillings (£1.50) for an army greatcoat and 30 shillings was worth having in those days.

I was to learn a lot about detention centres. These establishments are thought of as finishing schools for young gladiators. The army top brass send you there to break you and impose their will on you, so that if you love life too much, or fear violence too much, you are doomed – you are no longer a man but an army number and you will lend yourself to any act to get along. I have witnessed this with my own eyes. I've seen many broken men wince as an army screw walks by. If these broken men had not been so afraid of violence they would not have lost their manhood.

When I was nearing the end of my sentence a Scottish guy came in to serve a week or so for something or other. He was a real loud-mouthed, crude person, always boasting about the time he'd spent in Barlinnie Prison and the Gorbals. I knew instinctively that he was looking to have a shot at me. All the signs were there. I knew he had no nerve as he always bottled out of an eyeball confrontation with me. He would often make snide remarks about Cockneys and it was obvious he was saying these derogatory things in reference to me. Although nothing was said to my face he always made sure it was within my hearing, so I decided I would have to do him at the first opportunity. Even though I only had a few days left to serve I thought that if I marked him up enough I could be court-martialled with a dishonourable discharge at the end of it. So come tea-time I hit him full in the face with my enamelled metal drinking mug. Blood was spurting from his eye all over the place. As he keeled over I gave him a couple of kicks for good measure, left him in a crumpled heap and went back to my cell. I'm not ashamed of what I did and how I did it. It was forced on me and I had no option. It had to be done, for if I had not taken him out when I had the opportunity he would have taken me unawares.

As I lay on my bed in my cell I realised I would have to shelve my plans for the future and get a letter off to Ron telling him about this latest setback. I heard a lot of talking and heavy footsteps coming from outside my cell. I had left my cell door open but no one came near or by. After ten minutes or so I heard the guardsroom door slam so I assumed they had taken the Scotsman off to the MO or hospital to be stitched up. Several minutes later a couple of camp police came to my cell and asked, 'You OK, Billy?' I said, 'Yeah I'm fine.'

The following day I carried on as usual. No one commented on what I'd done, which I found all very confusing. Later on in the day, to my amazement, I learned that nobody claimed to have seen anything, which I thought was really big of them. The Scotsman claimed it was an accident and therefore was not pressing charges. I suppose by doing this he was saving face, which is understandable. He feared repercussions. The next couple of days went by smoothly enough. I think they realised I was provoked and had retaliated in the only way I knew how.

Once I was back with my regiment at the end of my detention I had no thoughts of staying put – my only problem was how to get back to London. Fortunately one of the officers was keen on boxing and had a good sense of humour. Although I had no plans of joining his boxing team and staying in the army he made things a little easier for me and appointed me his gardener, which was a joke really as his garden was only a little flower bed about six feet by two feet in front of his office. He asked me if I would consider joining his boxing team. I explained to him that I was out of shape. Finally I joined his boxing team as I knew I would at least get a few privileges and have all the time in the world to get myself fit.

My CO was a reasonable man who would always hear you out. I told him that I was anxious to get home and I would appreciate a weekend pass on compassionate grounds. After giving the request some consideration he gave me permission for a 48-hour pass. I think he realised it was most unlikely I would return. Within four days I was back in London. As soon as I arrived home I couldn't get out of army gear quick enough to put a clean shirt and suit on. Our house never had a bathroom so I went along to the public baths and spent ages in the bath until it got cold, then I went in for a swim in the swimming pool that was housed in the same building. I was feeling marvellously clean. Come evening Ron and I and several friends went to The Royal. For me it was the beginning of another 'holiday'.

I had only been on the run about a month when I was captured again. When I appeared in front of the magistrate I admitted to being a deserter and was remanded in custody to await a military escort. Once again I was taken by the military police to Old Scotland Yard. My shoe laces, belt and tie was taken off me and I was put in a cell to await my escort. The building was underground and the wooden floors were like polished glass. I could hardly breathe for lack of ventilation.

Shortly after I was installed in my cell a Red Cap opened the cell door and asked me if I would like some exercise. I thought the exercise would be beneficial and I was keen to get out of my cell as I was wide awake – I had been sleeping in the cell at the courthouse. The next thing I knew I was supplied with a heavy instrument they called a bumper which looked like a carpet sweeper but the handle was longer and the base was heavy with a cloth finish. The first step was to apply polish to the floor, then swing the bumper backwards and forwards. That was the only form of exercise apart from about half an hour in an enclosed yard. I should imagine the floor must have had the attention of thousands upon thousands of man hours over the years. No wonder it was like glass.

Eventually my escort arrived to take me back to Aldershot. I refused to be handcuffed and gawked at by people on the underground and I assured the corporal in charge of the escort that if they cuffed me I would fight every inch of the way. Knowing I was deadly serious, as I was, he agreed not to manacle me to an escort. Whilst we were going up the escalator at Waterloo to get to the main line station I pulled the corporal backwards so he landed on top of the other two. Then I sprinted up the stairs, crashed through the crowd and made good my escape through the busy station.

But my freedom was short-lived. Within minutes I had a crowd of people chasing me, including two police constables. I ended up with a twisted ankle up a blocked alley outside Waterloo station. I just accepted that escape was out and resigned myself to having handcuffs on. Within a couple of hours I was back in the guardroom at Aldershot. The following day I appeared in front of the Commanding Officer and was remanded. I was then put back in my cell. In the early hours of the morning whilst I was asleep the cell door was unlocked and three soldiers came in and started punching the life out of me. I managed to throw a couple of punches but I was overwhelmed. They gave me a good beating but made sure they didn't mark my face. The following day I appeared in front of the CO again and was further charged with assaulting a sergeant of the Seaforth Highlanders who was attached to our regiment. I later found out that the corporal who was in charge of the escort was a friend of the sergeant and because of my attempted escape he had been given a severe reprimand. It was a waste of time denying anything as the sergeant probably had years of untarnished service. I was eventually remanded in custody for a district court-martial.

Four or five weeks later my court-martial came up. I was allowed a defending counsel, but he was only a low-ranking officer. I think he believed my version of the assault but advised me against pursuing it. By now I was fed up and just wanted to get the court-martial out of the way and get on with my sentence. Under the circumstances my defence did well. He explained to the officers who sat in judgment that every time I deserted, my fellow soldiers would help themselves to my kit and subsequently I was pounds and pounds in debt. I was only sentenced to 84 days' detention, to be served at Colchester, and then returned back to the army to finish my national service. As I had been a deserter practically from day one I still had about two years to serve.

The following week I arrived at Colchester detention barracks and bedded down. Some of the screws there could make your life a misery and loved their power, especially the young ones. Prisoners never got pay but you were allowed two cigarettes a day, one at dinner-time and the other at tea-time. How it worked was that several huts would be used as dining-rooms and in each hut there were about ten tables, each for ten people. After your meal a screw would issue each man on the table with a cigarette and then light it for you. You were given about five minutes to smoke it, then when you were nice and giddy a screw would collect all the cigarette ends and count them to make sure nobody had walked off with one.

I was only there three days till I was in trouble for fighting with another prisoner and swearing at a screw who grabbed hold of me. I was awarded three days' punishment diet number one (PD1), or in layman's terms, bread and water for three days. The soldier I fought with was given a lesser sentence than me even though it was proved that he provoked me. He got punishment diet number two (PD2), which meant he was allowed porridge and potatoes for dinner, although he still had bread and water for breakfast and tea.

I don't recall meeting a decent screw in there, at least not a young one, although they left me pretty much alone. The screws were very much like a military police regiment and the regiment was named Military Provost Staff Corps. Some of the officers weren't bad, nor was the physical training instructor, but the doctor was a bit of an animal. One acquaintance of mine reported sick with migraine and he was excused duties for three days. Another soldier reported sick complaining of headaches and the doctor told him he was smoking too much and he was excused smoking for three days.

I always made a point of going about things in my own way. I tried to keep out of trouble, as the sooner I'd served my sentence the sooner I would be back in circulation again. I hated all the bullshit of cleaning your brasses and blancoing your webbing equipment but because I had gained quite a bit of respect in there some of the army prisoners did a lot of my kit cleaning for me. Most of the screws left me alone.

Eventually I got through my sentence and was sent back to my regiment. When I got there practically everyone knew I had just come from the detention barracks as the colour of the blanco used there was of a different colour to the regiment's. I had now been in the army nearly a year and had not even finished the basic training of 16 weeks – and I had no intention of doing so. At the first opportunity I would be back in The Smoke. I never bothered making any friends in the army as I had nothing in common with my fellow national servicemen. They were pretty friendly and civil to me but I preferred to be a loner – this way I was safer. As hard as it was for a person of my temperament, I bided my time and eventually got a weekend pass. Soon I was back in London and once more a deserter – naturally, I overstayed the weekend pass.

All the time I was a deserter I would spent a lot of time with Ron at The Royal dance hall. One time there I was getting a bit of aggravation and hostile stares from a big guy named Ronny Kingsnorth who headed a little mob from Wood Green. I knew this cold war had to come to a head and I badly wanted to do him. I knew he would be at The Royal on Friday evening so most of the Friday afternoon I sat in the back garden making a lethal cosh out of a 16-inch length of rubber hosepipe and stuffed and crammed about nine inches of it with pieces of lead until it was bulging. At the other end I crammed a round length of wood for a handle. The end product was a flexible weapon that would cause a lot of damage.

I told Ron to watch my back that night as I was going to do Kingsnorth. After we had been in The Royal a short time Kingsnorth arrived with his little team. I believe he realised it was his turn that night for he backed off. But I walked straight up to him and set about him with my tailor-made weapon. It caused a lot of damage but all of a sudden the lead I had crammed in became dislodged and was flying about everywhere. It was just like bullets flying about all over the place. However, the first few blows from my cosh had caused enough damage to Kingsnorth and he and his little mob fled. Ron thought it was hilarious when he saw the customers ducking for cover.

At about this time we met a man who lived on his own in a big house in Stamford Hill. His name was Johnny Abbott and meeting him was to lead to important things later on. Johnny Abbot was an elderly man who had been widowed or divorced. He was a bit of a weak character. His house was quite near the all-night cafe Ron and I used at Stamford Hill and his troubles started when he put a young couple up for the night whom he met there. Feeling a bit sorry for them, he offered them a bed, but within a couple of weeks his act of kindness turned into a nightmare as all their layabout friends from the all-night cafe wormed their way into the house and ate what food he had. None of them ever bothered paying rent or giving him a bit of money here and there.

These people were real liberty-takers and I'm sure Johnny Abbott was on the verge of a nervous breakdown. Although Ron and I seldom, if ever, got involved with people in the straight world, Ron really felt sorry for this old guy who, knowing our reputation, had poured his troubles out to him. Ron was a bit soft-hearted in some instances and told him we would go back with him to his house and sling them out. Johnny Abbott told us there would be about seven guys round there as well as the young couple. They were only dossers and drifters but they knew us by sight and reputation so they would be reluctant to make any resistance to our demands.

A friend of ours offered to drive us to the house in his old American car. Ron told him that people might get hurt but he insisted on coming along, which we appreciated as I was tooled up and didn't fancy getting a tug by the filth for carrying an offensive weapon. We all piled in the car. On arriving, Johnny Abbott used his street door key to let us in. The couple were sitting in the kitchen drinking tea. Ron and I marched into the kitchen and told them we wanted them out of the house now. The fella tried to talk Ron round so Ron gave him a backhander and told him to fuck off up north where he came from. He went pretty quickly and we soon turfed the others out. Our friend stayed outside with his car, holding a starting handle which must have been about three feet long. We thought a lot of this uncalled-for loyalty and he soon became a trusted member of our firm.

The Kray twins were conscripted into the army in 1952. A little while later, during one of my stints of desertion, friends told me they had both deserted and were anxious to meet me so I arranged to meet them in Shelley and Pepsi's restaurant in Tottenham. Shelley and Pepsi were brothers whom I had always got on well with and I often slung drunks and undesirables out for them. This was the first time I'd ever met the Kray twins on their own. The day of the meeting arrived and whilst I was just finishing a meal the Kray twins walked in and joined me at my table. They told me that soon after they had been conscripted they had gone absent without leave and been put in the guardroom. There they met another prisoner, Dickie Morgan, who was in the same regiment with the Krays when they were stationed at the Tower of London. He was an out-and-out thief who was much feared as a street fighter. When they were released from the guardroom the three of them had deserted together.

At first they had all stayed at Dickie Morgan's parents' house in Clinton Road in Bethnal Green. Dickie's father had just been sentenced for a raid on a warehouse where he was nightwatch-man and his brother, Chunky, was in prison. He was famous for the part he took in the Portland Borstal riot which was started by Frank Mitchell. Frank was a giant of a man whom I was to meet later.

I realised that this was a new way of life for them and they were finding it hard to handle. In me they saw an ally and someone to trust. I remember they seemed very naive as to how to live and, knowing I was a deserter, they asked me where I got money from. I could see that in me they saw a means of survival. During the whole time the twins were on the run they believed that the whole world as they knew it had come to an end. They were lost without their gang of little toughs to back them up and didn't have any clue as to how to make a living. Gone were the days when they could show their faces where they were known without fear of arrest.

The twins couldn't go on staying at Dickie's house because they were too well known in that area so they were looking for somewhere to live. They were relieved when I agreed to let them stay with me at a flat I'd rented in Finsbury Park. After we arrived at my flat they seemed pretty relaxed. The flat I had was one large room and a kitchen that I shared with the other tenants. The room was bleak and dreary with just two beds, a wardrobe and no chairs. It was always cold and we spent a lot of time sitting in the kitchen.

One of the other tenants was an old soldier and sometimes we might be sitting in the kitchen when the old soldier would come in and start reminiscing about his army days and what a good life it was, and tell us about all the action he had seen. We thought that he may have suspected we were deserters, as Finsbury Park was a predominantly Irish area and we were three young Cockneys of army conscription age, not working and coming in and out of the house at all times. We decided that it was better to move on and so we just walked out.

After that we spent most of our time in the West End and stayed nights at various places. Occasionally after it was dark we would creep into my mother's house or the Krays' house to stay for the night, but then we had to watch out because the police knew where our parents lived. Usually we would spend the night sitting up in Lyon's Corner House which was open 24 hours a day. We had no belongings with us and whenever I wanted a clean shirt or change of clothing I would slip home when it was dark and get spruced up. The twins had similar arrangements with their mother. Dickie Morgan would sometimes be there in the Corner House and we would all drink huge amounts of tea all night. To keep awake we would break open benzedrine inhalers and chew the tape inside which was saturated with benzedrine. In those days you could buy a benzedrine inhaler at the chemist's without a prescription. Sometimes we would take huge amounts of black bombers. There were all kinds of things to keep you awake and suppress your appetite.

I got on better with Reggie than Ronnie but I could see that Ronnie made all the decisions and spurred Reggie on. Reggie was always quite content just to live in Ronnie's shadow. Neither of them had any sense of humour and most of the time they were sullen and poker-faced. On one occasion, though, I had a spot on my nose and Ronnie made some offensive remark about it being contagious. I got angry and said, 'Well at least in a couple of days my nose will be normal. I won't be stuck with a boot nose like yours.' On hearing this, Reggie burst out laughing. Ronnie said to him, 'What are you fucking laughing at, you've got a bigger nose then me.' Then they started looking at their faces in the mirror at different angles. Ronnie does have a big nose and behind his back he was sometimes referred to as 'that boot-nosed bastard'. But mainly they were always talking about how they wished they were free men and walking down Bethnal Green Road without the fear of being arrested.

We met all sorts in Lyon's Corner House and would spend the night talking to them. At this time both twins always seemed anxious to please. They had hardly any money on them then and throughout the couple of years we spent together on and off as fellow fugitives they were always hard up. Sometimes we would spend three days and nights in the Corner House without a wink of sleep. The twins always seemed very vulnerable and on edge, especially Ronnie. He was always very withdrawn and had no conversation except 'yes' and 'no'. The only time he ever spoke a lot was about people he disliked and what they had done that he didn't approve of. Both of them had these peculiar low, soft voices. In fact, Ronnie always spoke as if he was whispering, but he did it in such a way that it scared most people. In a letter he wrote to me from prison years later he admitted that he was always badmouthing people. He said until he was 'certified insane' he had never known what friendship was. In the same letter he boasted that his life story had been written by the same writer who had written Ian Fleming's story and a history of the Dukes of Devonshire.

A friend of mine called Patsy Butler was in Borstal when the Krays first deserted from the army and when he heard they were on the run he escaped to join up with the twins and me as fugitives. Dickie Morgan was often with us so this made five deserters roaming London together. A lot of our time was spent in Mile End. Sometimes the five of us would stay at my mother's house or at the Krays' house, or at Dickie's mother's house in Clinton Road. She made us all welcome and let us come and go as we liked. She was an easy-going woman who never complained about having five deserters in her house. Nor did his overweight brother Chunky, who was now out of prison and living with his wife in the same house. We also spent a lot of time in a little cafe called the Orange Cafe in Burdett Road. It was while the twins were on the run from the army that they turned to real crime. Up till then it had been all show and glares, but now they really needed a way to make some money.

All types would congregate all night at the Corner House – crooks, prostitutes and, of course, homosexuals. It was when we were sitting up in Lyon's Corner House that I learned about Ronnie's homosexual tendencies. At first he kept this a closely-guarded secret as amongst other things it was still a crime to be a homosexual as well as being seen as effeminate and weak. But the Corner House was then the haunt of all kinds of fugitives, including many young runaway boys. Lots of these boys would spend the night at the Corner House and Ronnie Kray was always eyeing them up and down. Sometimes he would talk to them but there was always something so sinister about him that he made them feel uncomfortable and they would get away from him as soon as they could. There were a lot of gays in the Corner House in those days. Most were witty, especially one who was knocking on a bit and probably the most well-known queer in the West End. He (or she) was known as the 'Duchess' and he had spoken to Ronnie Kray a few times and knew instinctively that he was homosexual. Once when I was talking to the 'Duchess' I said, 'How are you so sure he's bent?' He said, 'It takes one to know one, and that's definitely a queen.'

Ron and I were still making the occasional trip to The Royal, Tottenham, though this was a bit dangerous for me as the dance hall is directly opposite the Tottenham Police Station. It was safe enough for the twins to frequent The Royal as they were not known by the Tottenham Police but I was. On a couple of occasions the twins would sleep at my home in Tottenham but this was a bit risky as the house was about a mile from The Royal and the bus service stopped early so it meant walking, and in those days you could get pulled by the Old Bill if you were walking late at night. Another added risk was that I seemed to get a lot of police visiting our house. I still had my street door key so one time at about 1 a.m. we let ourselves in. My mother and Speedy were out and my brother Ron told me they would probably be late. So we had to sort out the sleeping arrangements. The twins shared the same bed and were fast asleep when my mother arrived home. She guessed I was home so looked in the bedroom to see that I was OK. When she turned the light on and saw two identical people in bed she thought she was seeing things, what with the drink she had consumed. It must have been a bit of a shock.

Sometimes the twins and I went to their home so that they could get a fresh change of clothes. I got on well with the Krays' mother and father but I got the impression she never wanted the twins in the house for fear they would be arrested. She seemed to be expecting a knock on the door all the time. At this particular time Ronnie Kray had an Alsatian dog who most of the time was kept in the back garden. Ronnie liked to think that he was the only one who could handle the dog and thought the dog would only do things for him, so I used to wind Ronnie up by going out to the back garden and making a fuss of the dog. He seemed to forget that I too had Alsatian dogs of my own and his dog would be more interested in sniffing the scent of my dogs on my clothing. My two were called Rex and Sheba and they were very helpful if I had any problems with any of my benefactors. Benefactors are owners of premises who pay protection money. They also stopped me being pulled in by the Old Bill, for on one occasion when I was stopped by two constables who wanted to look inside the boot of my car, Rex and Sheba, who were moulting at the time, kept jumping up at the two policemen who got so covered with dog-hair that they decided not to bother to pursue whatever they had been chasing me for and go back to the station to clean themselves up.

The twins had both turned 19 now and I noticed Ronnie was getting more paranoid than ever and would lash out at anyone if they gazed too long at him or if someone was laughing and happened to look in his direction. Reggie was different entirely but he would always back Ronnie up even though he knew his twin was at fault. It was never a case of one on one.

All through the years when I was a deserter and a fugitive I always felt pretty safe in areas where I had not had any contact with the law. Anyway, I had false identification documents which would stand up to a check in the event of getting a pull. I had a driving licence and insurance cards for ID purposes in the name of Augustus Freeman. These forms of identification were needed at Lyon's Corner House, which was frequented by plain clothes police who would hang around the several entrances and challenge anyone who looked suspicious. In these surroundings the Krays would be a bit apprehensive, always thinking the army was going to jump out at them. The police were paid a bounty of seven shillings and sixpence (37½ pence) every time they pulled in a deserter, which says something about the value of a man to the state.

My old friend Tommy Etherington would sometimes join us in the Corner House. Another friend in those days was Tommy Smithson who was gambling mad. He was only a slightly built man and he never seemed to place much value on material things. He had started a spieler in Archer Street nearby and was doing well. Sometimes after spending all night in Lyon's Corner House Tommy would offer us the use of his spieler to get some sleep during the day when the club was closed. It was a gloomy place with a couple of snooker tables and some old tables and chairs. One of the snooker tables was used for shooting dice. The average spieler is mostly frequented by crooks, villains and habitual gamblers, and you also have a sprinkling of the local layabouts who treat it as a second home. In the smoke-filled atmosphere plans are hatched about various forms of villainy. In the summer months it reeks of body odour, which is not pleasant but somehow goes unnoticed.

The Krays always slept on the snooker tables but I preferred to sit in a chair and sleep as best I could rather than sleep on a slate-based table. Tommy's life revolved around gambling. I moved around with him for some time but he was never interested in long-range plans that needed time and preparation. He just ran with the pack (whoever they were) and was an out-and-out loner. He went through life with a non-caring attitude. He was always fighting and maybe losing, but as soon as his wounds were healed he would be back at his opponent's door for revenge. Over the years his face became scarred and battered. Tommy met his end in 1958 when he was shot in the stomach by one of the Maltese gangs. They say the Krays were very upset about Tommy's demise and even went to his funeral. This is typical of them, wanting to make a good impression on the underworld, but if Tommy had crossed them they'd have had him shot themselves. Tommy and I really got on well and occasionally I would spend the evening in a flat he shared with his girlfriend Faye.

One day I decided to drive round to see Johnny Abbott, as while I was away I'd been giving the old guy a lot of thought. I went to see him with Ron and when we arrived at his house and knocked on the door we saw him peering through the curtains. He welcomed us in and offered us tea or coffee but we declined. I asked if the people we had slung out had tried to return since I'd been away and he told me they had never bothered him, but shortly after they left he discovered that they had broken his electricity meter open and taken the money it contained and now the Electricity Board were looking to him to pay them or they would cut his electric supply off. Needless to say I gave him a few pounds to keep him going and then I had an idea. I needed to have a more regular income than I was getting so I asked him how he felt about having a spiel in his house of an evening until the early hours of the morning. I said I would organise the card schools and crap games, leave someone there so there would be no problems and insist that the cab drivers and other punters leave their vehicles at a distance from his house so there would be no complaints from the neighbours. He bought the idea and within the next few days we got half a dozen tables and several chairs delivered, as well as plenty of tea mugs. Within a month it was doing quite well, and everyone was happy, especially Johnny Abbott. This spieler was a great success for many years.

During all the periods when I was a deserter Ron and I spent a lot of time around the Cable Street area near Aldgate. Cable Street is only a stone's throw from Stepney Green where a lot of villains hang out. It was and still is a run-down, seedy place full of illegal gambling and drinking clubs where every form of vice is perpetuated. There was always a lot going on there – almost everyone there was into something. There were snooker halls, restaurants, cafes, clubs and, like Soho, nearly everything was open 24 hours a day. There were plenty of criminals but no organised crime, so making a few pounds here and there was no problem.

Cable Street was a pretty safe area for me as far as the Old Bill was concerned. Many of my friends from Stepney Green spent a lot of time there. Some came from what was called the Ocean Street estate. This was frequented by a mob of money-getters known as the Ocean Street Swells because they dressed smartly in tailor-made clothes. Ron and I had known the Ocean Street Swells from before I was forced into the army. In the beginning we had many rows and fights with them but we soon became the best of friends. They were not above a bit of skulduggery and helped us with anything we asked.

During the three years we moved around in Cable Street we made many friends from all walks of life, including restaurateurs, club owners and cafe proprietors. It was a rough area so a lot of these establishments needed some sort of protection which Ron and I organised for them. Even after I was kicked out of the army I returned to Cable Street and Soho because I had so many friends. In Cable Street it was inevitable that we also met many people who became our bitter enemies.

Around this time we were also spending a lot of time in the Aldgate area looking after a cafe-restaurant managed by Lionel Rose, who was to get nicked with me several months later in a stolen car. Things were running pretty smooth and we were getting a reasonable income. But we were getting a lot of aggro from the blacks who were pimping in Cable Street and in the Commercial Road area. They were not organised as such and each one was out for himself, and if any one of them was given the opportunity to coax one of his friend's hookers to work for him he would have no qualms or second thoughts about it. This led to a lot of arguing amongst themselves and fighting in which we had got involved, and this led to a bloody battle between us and the blacks.

A lot of people got hurt. After the battle we were sitting in Lionel's cafe with a few friends who had backed us up earlier when all of a sudden some plain clothes police officers entered and said they would like a word with us. The next thing we were carted off to Leman Street Police Station in three separate police cars. On arrival we were body-searched for weapons which fortunately we had left in our friend's car which by now was miles away. We were put in separate cells then called and questioned individually. By this time I realised our black opponents were being questioned and making statements. We denied being involved in any way.

It soon became clear that the spades were not pressing charges and we were allowed to leave. Several weeks later I learned that one of the blacks who was roped in had a warrant out for his arrest and was just as anxious to get out of Leman Street Police Station as we were. Although we wanted to keep a low profile as far as the police at Leman Street were concerned we had to stand our ground as the blacks would think they had seen us off. So we had to be seen large as life in and around the Cable Street area all the time. I was hoping the Old Bill would not start making himself busy as I got the impression he was a bit dubious about me and had suspicions aroused when I had to sign for the return of my personal property prior to release. I still had my ID papers in the name of Augustus Freeman and I had to stall a bit as I did not know at that time how to spell Augustus. So I just signed 'A' Freeman. I can see the irony now of using the name 'A Freeman' but at the time I was oblivious to it.

Ron told me I was probably magnifying the incident but if I wanted to I could stay off the manor and they would make a high profile in the places the plain clothes police were known to use. Unlike today you could spot them a mile off – nowadays it's not so easy to detect the plain clothes except that most of the unmarked cars they use are a dead giveaway, which leads you to believe that they really underestimate the mentality of the villains and criminals. I decided to take notice of Ron's view that I was probably making the incident bigger than it really was, so I decided to stay put on the manor with them most of the time.

Of course we never stayed in that area day and night as we had other things to attend to in other areas of London. We still had money coming in from our illegal spieler at Johnny Abbott's and we had a couple of cars at our disposal so we could cover a lot of ground, but we made a point that whenever we had reason to use both cars we would always keep a bit of distance between them, especially at night to avoid attention being drawn to us, although we very seldom had cause to use both cars together unless to show a bit of force or settle some dispute. I really wanted to keep a low profile but this was not always possible. There is always someone somewhere who causes a bit of aggravation or makes some disrespectful remark, so action must be taken to deter others and that action must be seen to be done.

Sometimes the twins and I would spend time in the Finsbury Park area and in the evening we visited an amusement arcade where we met some of the local young villains. The first two we met were also twins named Chris and Noel Flanagan and their constant friend nicknamed Jappy. He did resemble a Japanese person so I assume that's how he got his nickname. None of them ever did any work and they spent most of the day playing on the machines on the arcade. The Flanagan twins had a reputation as streetfighters although I never saw them in a fight.

The Krays were off by themselves most days and almost every evening Ron and I would go to Gray's dance hall in Finsbury Park. Every night some sort of fight would erupt there. Sometimes the Krays appeared there. It seemed as if they were canvassing all the London boroughs to make themselves known to local villains. This was so that they could count on support if they needed it but it also seemed like they were still looking for something in which they could get involved. One evening I left the hall early as I had arranged to meet my brother Ron. I spent some time with him and then made my way back to the twins. I imagine that while I was away they must have been talking things over as they told me that in the morning they were going to meet their uncle and go on the knocker with him again buying old clothes. We arranged to meet the following day in a pub in the City of London known as The 99. The shop where they sold the secondhand clothing was just round the corner from the pub and seeing it was situated in the City of London where the Kray twins were unknown to the police they were pretty safe.

I met them outside the pub and they both looked fairly smart with a change of clothes and clean shirts. I don't think they ever earned much money in the old clothes trade, but it was the only way they knew to make a living at that time. They used to argue quite a lot as Reggie always had more success on the knocker and he felt that Ronnie should make more effort. Sometimes they would have terrible rows. Reggie was always saying how fucking lazy Ronnie was just sitting in the car and leaving all the canvassing to him and their uncle. Although those rows were terrible the twins never came to blows. Very often during these arguments one or the other would try to draw me into it and get me to side with him but I would always remain neutral as I was smart enough to know that if I interfered they would more than likely both turn on me.

Neither of the twins was that smart, but Reggie was a bit brainier and quicker on the uptake than his brother. Ever since I've known him, Ronnie has had mood swings and was very paranoid, and as the years went by he became more so. In the beginning Ronnie would keep his homosexuality a closely guarded secret but after a few weeks he became open about it. He wasn't effeminate but I noticed that he held his cigarette in an odd effeminate way – a habit which he has to this present day, or at least he did the last time I saw him.

We used to have a lot of local opposition when we frequented Gray's dance hall in Finsbury Park and we were involved in many fights. A lot of this came about as a result of Ronnie Kray's paranoid disorder and the necessity he felt to prove that he was a superior being. It was because of this that I had a bit of an argument outside Gray's one night and cut one of the locals pretty badly with a tool he had tried to use on me and which he had dropped after I had punched him full in the face. I never really liked Gray's dance hall – there was no plushness or luxury about the place.

One day my brother had arranged for us to meet our cousin Chris in Hoxton Market where he had a greengrocer stall. The Krays came with us and we had a drink with Chris and a few of his friends in a local pub. The twins hardly said a word, but in the course of this meeting Jimmy Spinks' name was mentioned. Jimmy Spinks was one of the top local villains, feared in the Hoxton area. He was a hard case and he'd had so many battles that his face was covered in scars. There was a story about him that when a fish-and-chip shop owner tried to make Jimmy pay for his fish and chips, Jimmy threw the shop cat into the fish-fryer. When his name came up the twins made it known that they would like to know where he lived or where he could be found. So I took them along to Spinksy's house as I knew him quite well.

We knocked on the door and were asked in. The twins seemed very nervous. All of a sudden Ronnie Kray asked Jimmy if he could get him a gun. I was a bit surprised as we had no arguments with anyone that would warrant the use of a gun. I suppose we had made a few enemies along the way but I think Reggie was as surprised as me. I don't suppose for one minute Jimmy would have helped even if he could as the Krays were complete strangers and no one in their right senses would put his liberty on the line like that. The man was no fool. After we left Jimmy's we went back to Mile End to the cafe in Burdett Road. Shortly after that I realised Ronnie had got a gun from somewhere, and always carried it.

CHAPTER FIVE

More of the Same

Ron and I took a flat in Harringay but within two weeks of moving in I was captured. So once again I was in front of the magistrate admitting to being AWOL, remanded for a military escort, taken to Old Scotland Yard by the Red Caps and banged up until the escort arrived to collect me and take me back to the barracks. The following day I was cuffed to an escort and appeared in front of the Commanding Officer charged with being absent without leave and remanded in custody for two days. When I made my next appearance once again half my kit was stolen so I was even deeper in debt. I thought this time I was looking at a year in the detention barracks, which did not worry me for I was sure to get a dishonourable discharge at the end of it.

The CO to my surprise only gave me 28 days' detention which he allowed me to serve in the guardroom. This suited me fine as the guardhouse was OK and most evenings the guard commander would unlock my cell and I would spend most of the night sitting round and talking to the guards or playing cards and showing them some card tricks.

None of my family knew I had been captured so I sent a letter saying I was back in custody. I really got on well with the officers.

They treated me with respect. I believe they realised I was caught up in something that was not of my making and I seriously think they went out of their way to make life easier for me. I in turn respected them for making allowances.

A few days after I had been in the guardroom I was surprised to find I had a visitor. When I looked up from my bed I was pleased to see my mother standing in my cell with my cousin Patsy's husband, Punchy Hines, and two of his friends who had driven my mother by car all the way down from London to Aldershot to see me. She told me later that the drive down was a bit of an ordeal as Punchy Hines and his two friends were bank robbers and blag merchants and on the way down they frequently stopped to case future targets to knock over. This caused my mother a lot of anxiety, as she thought that when they were stopping to case the post offices and so on they were going to commit the robbery there and then.

I really enjoyed the visit as all the camp police were civil and made us cups of tea. Halfway through the visit cousin Punchy pulled me aside and whispered if I wanted out. I said I appreciated the fact that he was willing to put his liberty on the line to get me out but I was quite content to serve my sentence and get my discharge. I said I would soon be back in London and he would be the first one I would look up.

On reflection, if I had the choice I would have preferred to spend the duration of my national service in the guardroom. Most of the time I would spend in my cell lying on my bed. Occasionally a decent guard commander would be on duty and would socialise a bit. One day a lance corporal tried to put a bit of a scare up me by saying that I could end up being Shanghaied. I'd never heard this word before so I asked him what he meant. He told me that when the army had difficult soldiers who were constantly in trouble they would put the cuffs on them and ship them abroad. After giving this matter some thought I said, 'Well it won't happen to me as I've not yet passed my 16 weeks basic training so stop trying to be so fucking smart.' This was a fact. I had not yet finished my basic training and never did. But I am told that this practice of putting problem soldiers in handcuffs and shipping them off to some far-off posting overseas did occasionally happen.

Although it was not a recognised thing to have visitors whilst in the guardroom, Ron would often drive down with a couple of pals to visit me. There were no facilities for visiting purposes but the officers were always obliging and I was allowed to spend some time with Ron, who would tell me all the news of what was happening and who was doing what. But most of all I was pleased to have him visit me as he had a great calming influence on my life. Nothing was too much for him to do in order to make my lot better. I always knew in my heart that if it came to it Ron would put his life on the line for me, which I believe he finally did. But we will come to those acts of self-sacrifice later. Life in the guardroom was pretty soft and I was left pretty much alone.

As usual, as soon as I'd finished my stint in the guardroom I took the first opportunity to leg it back to London. It was good to be back with Ron again and catch up with the news. After we had had a few drinks in The Royal we decided to go to Stamford Hill and see some friends and have a salt beef sandwich, so we all piled into a friend's car. We got there just as the Salt Beef Restaurant was closing but we were given a table with no fuss and tucked into our meal. After the meal we crossed over to the all-night cafe. It was really pleasant to be back – everyone was pleased to see me, as I was them.

We were getting quite known now and accepted. Occasionally I would get a pull from a couple of plain clothes Old Bill but I always made sure I had some form of identification in another name. Insurance cards could be bought on the streets. Ron and I still spent a lot of nights in the Corner House. One of the regulars there was a character named Johnny Hudson from Covent Garden. He was an ex-boxer who often put on unlicensed boxing shows, mostly out of London. He was always looking for boxers of all weights. He knew I'd boxed as an amateur and asked me if he could put me on the list, to which I agreed. I made quite a bit of money by fighting in a few matches.

Another person who used to spend some time in Lyon's was a fella called Curly King, who came out of Bow or thereabouts. I never had any time for him as he was really flash. He must have been in his mid-twenties and would run a little gang of teenagers who really thought he was the business. He also used to go to The Royal with his gang of little boys. Curly did a lot of boxing. I got on really well with Johnny Hudson and told him to get Curly King on the bill as my opponent. In the meantime I'd had a talk with Curly and assured him that we would just be more or less sparring and pulling the punches and it would be a good day's outing. I was looking forward to the event which was about a week away. In the meantime we were sleeping in Tommy Smithson's spieler.

The Krays were also booked to box for Johnny Hudson, but a couple of days before the tournament they nearly got captured. They were spending a lot of time in a snooker hall near Dickie's mother's house and years later they took it over. They also spent a lot of time in the Orange Cafe round the corner, drinking endless cups of tea. Coming out of there on a foggy day they ran straight into an Old Bill who knew them and in making good their escape they had manhandled him, so they decided to give the tournament a miss as they had to be more cautious. They were now wanted for assaulting a police officer as well as for desertion. This meant that the Krays' stomping grounds were restricted. They could not show their faces in Mile End or spend the occasional night at their parents' home. If they had split up they would have had more chance but this they would not do as on their own they would be vulnerable to the many enemies they had accumulated.

Finally the day of the boxing tournament came round. By now Curly King was aware I had the hump with him and was putting himself out to be nice to me prior to our bout which, although he never realised it, made my inner feelings of dislike for him worse. Now I despised his grovelling. Our bout lasted two rounds as he refused to come out for the third. This contrasted with the last occasion I boxed for Johnny Hudson when the tablets I had taken to keep awake were just wearing off. I'd had no sleep for two nights and I could hardly keep my eyes open even though I was boxing. I managed to go the distance but lost on points.

All this time I was still moving round the West End and spending a lot of time with Tommy Smithson in his spieler. I was an asset to Tommy as my knowledge of craps and other games of chance was considerable. Shortly after my brother Ron left our home to join me. The Krays were still in touch with us and appeared to like Ron a lot now that they had got to know him. He had set up his own snooker hall and gaming club and they were impressed about the set-up he had. I realised that the true reason my Ron had for leaving home to join me was that he had heard, as most people had, about the Kray twins' vicious unprovoked attacks that were snowballing and he knew I was vulnerable on my own. I was pleased to have Ron around as he was good company and humorous.

In those days in the Corner House Reggie would pretend to me and his twin brother that he too had homosexual tendencies and liked young boys but I realised he was probably doing this so that I could not discriminate against Ronnie and he would find favour in Ronnie's eyes. If Ronnie saw a young boy he liked he would be very attentive and polite. He never held the boy's hand or made contact in any way, so to all around the outward appearance would be quite normal and his secret would remain hidden. Whenever he met a boy to whom he was attracted he would always refer to him as a 'prospect' and that word would let us know what he meant. Sometimes he might spot a boy on the other side of the road and say, 'He's a nice prospect.' Reggie and I would know what he meant but whoever was in our company was unaware of what the word implied. In private Ronnie would say about a boy, 'Hasn't he got a nice compact little bum?', or, 'He's got nice long eyelashes.' Reggie would always be in agreement and play up to him.

I remember one night when the twins and I were in Lyon's Corner House in the early hours of the morning waiting for Tommy Smithson. While we were waiting I was talking to one of the regular customers. He was one of the characters of the West End known as Yossell, who had a dark brown hat always worn in Harry Lime's style in the film *The Third Man*, starring Orson Welles. Yossell was a racing man and a gambler who, when he was not in Lyon's Corner House, was in the billiard hall in Great Windmill Street near Piccadilly having a side bet on one or two of the games being played. Whilst we were talking to Yossell, Ronnie Kray noticed a young, dark-haired boy sitting on his own at a table nearby. Ronnie Kray nudged me saying, 'Look at that nice prospect.' Within a few minutes the kid had joined us at our table and Ronnie Kray was fawning all over him and buying him cups of tea and cakes. I thought surely this kid must realise why he's receiving all this attention. Eventually Tommy Smithson turned up and we all went back to Tommy's spieler with the young boy in tow. Ronnie and the boy ended up sleeping together on a billiard table whilst Reggie and I sat in chairs nodding off – or at least I was, but Reggie was high on pills. All night long between my naps I could hear Ronnie Kray's muffled voice talking to the young boy. Proper sleep was impossible for me that night! After that incident we always made sure we never brought any young boys along if we were meeting with the twins. Although Ronnie Kray was a bit peeved about it all we continued to see them on and off though we always avoided discussing any business matters of any sort with them. But then I would seldom if ever take anyone into my confidence apart from my brother Ron.

We never severed relations with the Krays completely as we would often meet up with them and spend a day or two together and then go our separate ways, but soon after this the Krays went back to the same cafe where they had assaulted the Old Bill. Someone saw them and they got nicked and charged with assaulting a police officer. They were given a month each which they served in Wormwood Scrubs. Then the army got them again and they did nine months detention in Shepton Mallett. It was in Shepton Mallett that they met Charlie Richardson. In about 1954 the twins were dishonourably discharged.

In those years the West End was like a magnet. During the times I spent there I met a vast amount of characters. Some of them were of my own calibre and sadly some are no longer with us, having been shot, stabbed or died in accidents. But many have remained lifelong friends together with all the others I have acquired along the way.

I was well past 20 now. My brother had gone home to spend a few days with our mother and to sort a problem out we were having with a couple of patrons at an illegal spieler we were operating. I had arranged to meet Ron at Stamford Hill on the Friday evening. I was with a couple of pals from Mile End, East London, and we had arrived early in order to have a meal in the E & A Salt Beef Restaurant. As we walked into the restaurant I noticed a young guy who had been in my regiment and had now finished his national service. On one occasion he had been one of the military escorts sent from my barracks to take me back to the unit. He was really awkward and flash at the little bit of power he had on this occasion. When he saw me walk into the E & A he went white as a sheet and made a pretence of a smile, hoping I would forget the incident – but it was all fresh in my mind.

I stood at the bar for some time just looking at him. I noticed he had a friend with him who looked over at me whilst the ex-escort was talking to him and they were both looking really worried. His friend was worrying in vain as I had no score to settle with him. I walked over to their table and told the ex-escort to eat his meal as we had some unfinished business to settle. He then began grovelling and making excuses, saying he was only doing his duty and then insisting that it had been the other two escorts who were awkward at my request to be allowed to make a phone call to let my brother know I had been picked up, but I knew it was he who had done all the objecting. His friend then spoke, saying he didn't want to get involved as it was none of his business, so I replied, 'Yes, I know. But in future you want to be more particular about the company you keep.' I wanted to give him a belting there and then but the owner of the E & A was a friend of mine and I am not without principles, so I left their table saying, 'Just finish your meal – I haven't got all night', and walked back to join my friends at the bar. I told them what went on at the table and why I was so angry.

By now Ron had arrived with a pal. I told him about the situation and when we looked over to their table they were both as white as a sheet and so scared it was pathetic. Ron thought it was really amusing and said I would be taking a liberty if I gave him a beating as he was a skinny runt and there were other ways. Just then his friend came over and once again explained to my brother his position. He said that he never knew his friend all that well but he would like us to have a drink with him.

By this time there was an atmosphere about the place. It had not gone unnoticed when I went to their table and the other customers had heard my threats. We could have told his friend to leave there and then but if we did he would probably get on the phone to the police. I was by now simmering down a bit, but I thought it was a cheap shot to try and bribe us to save his own skin by the price of a drink and I told him as much but assured him he was safe and that no harm would come to him. I told him to go back and join his friend. Ron told me to forget it. By now I had calmed down as Ron had a great influence on me so the five of us sat down and had a meal in the restaurant. In other circumstances the outcome would have been quite different, had the confrontation taken place other than at a friend's premises. So the ex-escort had a narrow escape.

We used to spend a lot of time at Stamford Hill and made many friends. I was still seeing my teenage friend Tommy Etherington, who fortunately was not conscripted into the army and missed his national service on medical grounds. I don't know what stroke he pulled to avoid getting drafted into the army as he was A1 physically and mentally. I vividly remember his mother, who is no longer with us, with great affection and appreciation as she was always kindness itself towards me throughout my bouts of desertion. She would always leave the ground-floor front-room window unlocked so that I was sure of a place to sleep.

CHAPTER SIX

Maltese Joe

We were still doing good business in Cable Street and by now the trouble that we had with the black opposition had run its course and things were pretty tranquil. What was worrying me at the time was that far too many people knew I was a deserter from the army and some of them I had had reason to physically hurt. I knew it was not beyond these people to grass on me to the police and get me off the streets and out of circulation. So we were moving about different areas quite a lot and very few people knew where I would be at any specific time. I trusted only the people I was closely involved with but even that only to a degree.

Cable Street is infested with Maltese and blacks, many of whom are pimps. But there is no allegiance among them as they are all in competition with each other. This is also true of the Notting Hill and Paddington areas where Rachman made his fortune. When runaways leave home many of them suffer what I consider to be the three worst things in life – cold, hunger and loneliness. Any young runaway girl is vulnerable to anyone who wants to exploit her and a pimp is a master of this. So when the pimp offers a girl his friendship she will grab this token of kindness and caring. In many ways I am old-fashioned and believe implicitly that women are the weaker sex and more vulnerable to affairs of the heart.

It was in the Cable Street area in the early 1950s that I first met Maltese Joe, a well-known pimp. I disliked the man intensely and would go out of my way to antagonise him. Maltese Joe had no organisation like the Messina brothers who imported girls from all over the world and had the police eating out of their hands. Maltese Joe's girls were just street-walkers operating around Commercial Road, Bayswater Road and Cromwell Road.

During one of my visits to Lionel Rose's cafe in Cable Street with my brother we noticed Maltese Joe scolding a young girl aged about 17. She was in tears and kept saying to him, 'Please leave me alone, just leave me alone.' Ron and I were behind the counter with Lionel Rose and the girl kept looking, pleading, in our direction. As there were some other Malts in the cafe, I told Ron to watch my back and I walked over to the girl and Maltese Joe. I noticed that Ron said something to the other Malts. I didn't hear what he said but they made a hasty exit.

When I got to their table I ignored Maltese Joe and said to the girl, 'Are you OK?' She was frightened out of her life and asked if she could join us. So I told her to go over to where Ron was. I was seething by then and said to him, 'Why are you causing this girl all this grief?' And he said, 'We were just having a bit of an argument.' Then he had the cheek to say, 'It's none of your business.' At this I grabbed him by the shirt collar, head-butted him straight in the face and said, 'Well, I am making it my fucking business.' Then Ron left the girl with Lionel Rose and joined us. He said to Maltese Joe in his most menacing voice, 'You get out *now* and if you cause us any more problems, I will personally castrate you and you'll be no good for any woman, man or beast.' Maltese Joe went white and left. After he had made his rapid exit from the cafe I joined Ronnie and Lionel and we asked the girl what the problem was between her and the Malt. She told me that she knew he was a ponce and he was insisting on looking after her. We could see she was hungry so we bought her a sandwich and a cup of tea.

Her name was Margaret and she lived in Thornton Heath. She said her father was a bus-driver and very strict. Her mother always took her father's side in all things and she had left home to get a job in one of London's hotels on a living-in basis. In a way I felt responsible for the girl as to an extent I had got myself unwittingly involved, so I asked her if she would agree to me taking her home the following weekend. She agreed and meanwhile, seeing she had nowhere to live, it was arranged for her to stay with Connie Munn's girlfriend, Joan, who lived with her parents off the manor.

The following Sunday I picked the girl up from Joan's and drove her to her parents' home. I met the parents and explained the girl was in some danger. They kept looking at me and then at Big Connie in the car, not knowing where I fitted in or what my role was. Her father seemed a real fucking tyrant whom I could have cheerfully strangled. I felt sorry for the girl as her petty tyrant father laid down the rules and regulations that she must abide by. Her mother never said a word and not one word of thanks was given. I felt relieved when we left but the reunion was not what I expected it to be. As we drove off I looked back at their house and their neat and well-tended garden then told Connie I needed some refreshment and we stopped at a pub for a drink. I often wondered what became of the girl – she seemed to be caught between the devil and the deep blue sea and I was glad to have been able to help her even for a few days.

A week or so after we had returned the girl to her parents we heard Maltese Joe and a couple of his friends had wrecked Lionel's cafe because we had helped the girl. At this time the Malt had a yard in Cable Street where he kept a couple of old cars and a large American Ford Fairlane. This yard was just a front to hide his pimping activities. After wrecking the cafe he went into hiding and kept away from his usual haunts. As soon as we heard what he had done we decided he had to be dealt with severely – he had to have a couple of limbs broken. So we searched high and low for him. But our vengeance had to wait for a couple of days because together with Lionel Rose and another fella I was nicked in a stolen car. The registration number of the car had been changed but we ran straight into a road block put up by the Old Bill.

In order to get my friends off the hook I told the police that at no time were they aware that the car was hot. But they wouldn't buy it and we were all charged with car-theft. Things couldn't have been worse for in the boot were a couple of tyre levers which could be classed as lethal weapons. The result was we each got six months' imprisonment.

I was annoyed at getting nicked at that particular time as one of our close pals had just taken a beating and got cut by Maltese Joe and a couple of his Maltese friends. We had made plans to settle the score that weekend and knew where they would all be at a particular time but here I was stuck in a cell. By now Ron must have realised I'd got captured but I had no way of getting word to him.

I was hauled in front of the magistrate at Thames Court, East London, and looked around the court in the hope that I would see someone I knew who could get a message to Ron to let him know what happened. Alternatively I was hoping one of my two pals I was nicked with would be allowed bail, but it was not to be – we were each remanded in custody for a week. I was put in Pentonville along with my pals.

As soon as I got there I wrote a letter to Ron telling him what had happened and the date I was due to appear in front of the magistrate for sentence, so that he could see me and we could reorganise various plans we had in the pipeline. The week in the Ville wasn't too bad as I knew quite a few other cons from the outside. I was anxious to get word to Ron. I could not be sure my reception letter would reach him in time as I did not know how long it would be in the censor's office. Eventually I found a con who was due to be released the following day, so I told him where to find Ron and assured him Ron would reward him financially for his troubles and that he would be doing me a personal favour. I got the impression he was a drifter with nothing or nobody on the outside waiting for him so I was pretty sure he would do what I asked.

The week went by without any notable incident and I spent most of the time behind the door. Because I was convicted and not yet sentenced I was given a job in the dismantling shop sitting at a table with other cons and a few old lags taking pieces of electrical equipment to pieces with a screwdriver. I didn't mind this as I sat next to a couple of guys that I had met on the outside.

After the week in custody expired the three of us were back at Thames Magistrates Court and put in separate cells. Shortly after I was installed an army lieutenant appeared at my cell door. I was a bit surprised at his frankness and the hospitability he offered as I'd really given the army a lot of headaches. He offered me a cigarette but I declined. I got the impression he did not relish any of his day's duty but I was thankful he spared me a lecture. Soon the three of us were in the dock. The magistrate, who was an ex-colonel, didn't waste much time with me after the lieutenant had said his piece. He gave me six months. I had spotted Ron and a couple of pals in the public gallery. I motioned for him to see me downstairs in the cells. As I left the dock to start the six-month sentence I glanced up at the lieutenant who looked a bit despondent about it all, so I gave him a wink which brought a smile to his face. Ron came down to the cells to visit me. I wasn't really surprised to see the guy whom I'd met in the Ville and asked to get in touch with Ron. Like me, Ron felt this man could be trusted to a degree so he fixed him up with a roof over his head at Johnny Abbott's in return for making himself useful. His name was Scouse Eddie and he was a likeable person who originated from Liverpool but had drifted around London for many years in between doing bits of bird.

When Ron was visiting me in the cells we agreed that we still had to sort things out with regard to the aggro we were having with the little Maltese mob but unfortunately I could not take part due to my spell of imprisonment. But I stressed the point to Ron that they would have to make sure they sorted them out good and proper in order to make an example of them and also try to keep my whereabouts from any enquirers – the less that's known the better. It could more than likely be to our advantage if I went missing for the time being. This might cause a bit of confusion – they would wonder what I was concocting as Ron and I were seldom apart. So it was of the utmost importance that they and others thought I was at large rather than in the slammer.

Within a short time our visit was at an end and I was taken to the Ville to start my sentence. I was fortunate enough to have a cell with two other cons. Being C of E, I had a white cell card on a board outside my cell – Roman Catholics had red cards, other faiths had various coloured cards. Written right across my cell card was 'To be detained at Gate' which meant that when I had served this sentence the military police would be waiting outside the prison gates and I would in due course have another court-martial and more detention. The army would want its pound of flesh after this present sentence had expired. So I was not too anxious to go back and was quite content to stay in prison. I made sure I lost a lot of remission for brawling and refusing to work.

I wasn't surprised to find myself allocated a job in the mail-bag shop, making mail-bags by hand with needle and waxed thread. I knew quite a few cons from outside in the mail-bag shop so I was kept up to date with what was going down and who was doing what. What wages I earned sewing mail-bags were a pittance but I lived better than most cons in there and as soon as I arrived in the prison I was installed in the prison's so-called élite circle. Prisons are pretty much the same as the world outside with its upper class, middle class and lower class which consists of drunks, vagrants and gas meter bandits. Even the screws are aware of who's who and leave you pretty much alone. Of course there is always the exception who is normally a young, green and keen rookie eager to exert the new-found power bestowed on him.

After about a week had passed Ron and a couple of pals visited me. I was pleased to learn that Ron and a couple of our mob had done Maltese Joe, cutting him pretty badly, distributing a few stitches out to his pals and smashing his big American convertible to smithereens. Scouse Eddie had volunteered to go along and help even though we barely knew him. I was particularly pleased to learn that Eddie was a good streetfighter and gave a good account of himself. I told Ron to be sure to bring him up on the next visit as I was impressed at the allegiance he had shown just because we had given him a roof over his head, a bit of money in his pocket and some decent clothing on his back. It was good to hear that things were ticking over nicely but disappointing to know that practically everyone we were having dealings with knew I was in the slammer. I suppose it was inevitable that it would become common knowledge sooner or later but I would have preferred it to have been just a little later.

It seemed that as soon as the visit had got under way it was time to say our goodbyes, but I was left with the knowledge that Ron had wasted no time in settling our account with Maltese Joe and that the American car which was his pride and joy was a wreck. Knowing him he probably only had third party insurance if any, and the local police must have quietly been delighted as they knew he was pimping and he was flash with it. After the visit I went back to the mail-bag shop elated at all this good news.

However, it was always at the back of my mind that after this spell in the slammer I would have to spend more time in the guardroom awaiting my court-martial. The next month went by without much incident except I lost three days' remission and got put in the chokey block (solitary confinement) for three days for so-called insolence against a screw. Basically what it boiled down to was that he didn't go a bundle on me nor I on him and he would go out of his way to antagonise me by repeatedly taking my cell card off the board, making out to read it, then putting it back. I knew he was winding me up and by then I'd had enough of his antics. One afternoon as I neared my cell to get banged up for the night he was standing there just looking at my cell card which said, 'To be detained at Gate'. I could see by the way he was looking at me that he was winding me up about this so I took the card out and stuffed it under his nose shouting, 'What the fucking hell's the matter with you? Can't you read or what?' Within minutes all hell broke loose and half a dozen screws jumped on me.

Next morning I was up in front of the Governor on report. I know from past experience it's futile to argue the toss – you can't win but you at least retain your dignity which in a manner of speaking makes you a winner if you keep your cool. I didn't mind it too much in the chokey block as I was under no pressure and I could start thinking straight. I had no plans of serving any more time in any army detention establishment if I could help it. But I would cross that bridge when I came to it.

Soon I was back on the wing. The month went by without any notable incident. I had sent a visiting order out to Ron and was anxious to get news in depth as to what was happening. Although I was getting plenty of mail all the letters incoming and outgoing were censored, so discretion was called for. Shortly after sending the visiting order out I was called out of the mail-bag shop for the visit. I was surprised to see that Ron had brought a stranger along even though he knew I was against talking openly about our personal involvements. I was openly annoyed and asked Ron why he'd brought him up to see me. I could see the fella was a bit uncomfortable and Ron, knowing I was annoyed, told me to listen carefully to what this stranger had to say as it would be to my benefit. I looked the guy over – he was pretty well dressed in a conservative way but without the bowler hat and umbrella. At the time I was thinking that maybe this fella was some sort of fraudster or he was going to let us into some sinister business venture so I became attentive and anxious as to what was coming next.

He started by telling me there was a good chance that I could get my dishonourable discharge from the army at the expiration of the present sentence I was serving. There would be no military escort waiting for me at the gate. He went on, telling me in detail what I must do. He told me that at the first opportunity I should make an appointment to see the Prison Governor and ask for permission to write to the Home Secretary and send a written petition asking that the army grant me a discharge.

At the end of the visit I thanked him for coming to see me. I felt really excited and lost no time in asking to go on Governor's Report. All weekend I sat in my cell writing on scraps of paper. What I should write and how best I could present my situation came extremely difficult for me as at that time in life I was a cripple when it came to reading, writing and spelling. So many of my schooldays had been lost due to the Blitz. Besides which I was a habitual truant and spent most of my childhood chasing the elusive dollar – paramount importance in those days as our mother used to find it really difficult to make ends meet. Although she never mentioned it, we knew. I was thankful though that I had all weekend in front of me so that I could present some sort of reasonable petition to support my claim for a discharge.

I settled the issue in front of me by stating the undisputable facts that were recorded on army records. I pointed out that up until now I had spent over three years fighting the army. I had had two court-martials and spent numerous months in army detention centres and weeks in the guardroom, so it must be obvious that theirs was a lost cause. I could take all they handed out and more so I respectfully asked that they give consideration to my petition as I am a most determined person. As soon as my cell was unlocked on the Monday morning I made an application to see the Prison Governor. I explained the situation to him and was given permission to petition the Home Secretary at the Home Office. I wrote out a petition and handed it in, then I put the matter out of my mind and carried on as usual.

I told a few of my pals that I had put in a petition. They all thought I had a good chance. After a while I began to regret saying anything to my buddies about it as it was always the topic of conversation in the exercise yard. Everyone seemed to think it was a certainty, which made me start building my hopes up. When I thought back at all the trouble I had put the army to I reckoned I must be odds on. But I would not allow myself to believe that it was an open and shut case. In my mind I still thought there was someone somewhere who would think I was able to be made into army material – there is always a joker in the pack.

As far as I was concerned this private war I was waging against the army was not of my making. If I had volunteered then I would be at fault but I did not offer my services, so therefore I was not at fault. I think on the whole the officers that I had come in contact with could identify with my lot, so I respected them. But to the average NCO I was looked on as a troublemaker. I think what I found most humiliating was the thought of being given orders by an NCO who, because he had a couple of stripes, thought he was my superior. Some of them probably enlisted in the army because they could not make anything of themselves in civilian life. Or maybe the crux of the matter was that I was a leader not a follower, and here I was stuck in the army with a bunch of people with whom I had nothing in common. I honestly could not understand why the army had not relinquished its grip on me. Surely they must realise that the War Office was fighting a losing battle. In another era or under other circumstances things might have worked out differently.

Now that I had put in my petition time seemed to have stood still but the days slowly turned into weeks and the weeks into months, by which time I had almost forgotten and resigned myself to another court-martial. My present term of imprisonment had nearly run its course. I was thinking I would probably get about 12 months' detention, in which case I would be free in about a year's time, so things weren't so bleak. I was still getting a monthly visit by Ron apart from the one time he came to visit me and I was in the chokey block. His visit then was not permitted.

Three days after my solitary confinement had come to an end Ron came to visit me and gave me all the news of the latest developments. It seemed things were still ticking over nicely. We never spoke about the petition as he knew this was a sore point with me now. I was pleased he had come on his own as I had a lot of personal things to tell him, besides which it was nice to have Ron all to myself even though it was only for a brief time. As always, the visit went so fast many things were left unsaid. We bid our fond farewells and went our separate ways.

A few days after the visit with Ron I was in the mail-bag shop deep in conversation with one of the cons whom I'd known from the outside when a screw came into the workshop. I knew him quite well and always got on well with him. He had some sort of job in the administration office. He nodded an acknowledgment to me and came over to tell me to report to the Governor in the morning. I realised it could only be in relation to my petition to the Home Secretary. When I got back on the wing I was told the same thing by the PO (Principal Officer). I made sure I kept it to myself as by now I was fed up with all the speculation and opinions of the cons.

The morning came and I was beckoned into the Governor's office. He had a bundle of official-looking papers in front of him and started by saying, 'Webb, I have a reply received yesterday from the Home Office regarding the petition you wrote some time ago.' He went on and on and I can't remember the exact words but it seemed unending. He said that after two and a half years, two court-martials for desertion, assaulting a sergeant in the Seaforth Highlanders and a lot of other stuff, the army had decided that no amount of spells in detention barracks or army prisons would ever work and I was to be dishonourably discharged. At this point he showed me the copy which read: 'This man has found it hard to conform to military discipline and it is recommended that he be discharged with ignominy: Military Conduct = Indifferent.'

On hearing this news I was elated. I was going to ask for a special visit but I guessed it would be refused so I asked for a special letter instead, which was granted. Now I could really put the plans I had shelved into practice. By now I had less than two weeks to serve so I got the special letter off to Ron telling him I'd won my private war with the army. The next few days sped by. I received a letter from Ron saying he would pick me up outside the prison at 7.30 a.m. on the day I was released. The day before I was to be released I gave all my personal belongings to my pals as was the standard practice in prison.

When I look back on my life as a solider, or rather a permanent deserter, I have many good memories. I met many good people. Ronnie Kray once wrote to me from Parkhurst Prison saying he would never forget those hard times when we were deserters together. I think in those days as a deserter the good times outweighed the hard times. Being on the run wasn't easy. There are many unscrupulous characters around who look for an easy mark and would rob you of your teeth and then come back for your gums. But all in all I made a lot of good friends and my time 'in' the Army was something to look back on.

CHAPTER SEVEN

A Legitimate Scam

The following morning Ron and a couple of pals were there outside the prison on the dot. I couldn't get in the car quick enough as all my suit was creased where it had been left in a parcel for several months. I was longing to see our mum whom I had not seen during my time in the slammer. I had forbidden Ron to bring our mother on a visit as seeing me locked up would only make her sad. I would write to her at every opportunity and tell her all was fine and paint the screws as fatherly figures who were always ready to help and give advice. I certainly could not and would not give our mother any cause for concern or discomfort, nor would Ron as we idolised her. When speaking of her we would always refer to her as our mother or our mum. Never at any time would we refer to her as our old lady or our old girl.

Naturally at that time in the morning the traffic was heavy owing to the rush hour so it seemed to take an eternity getting home. As I went through the front door I was surprised to find Reggie Kray in the kitchen waiting to welcome me back. Our mother prepared a nice breakfast for the four of us. I had taken great pains to make myself as neat and tidy as possible (under the circumstances) and I was pleased when she remarked how well I looked. Speedy, who had married our mother when I was about 17, was at home and pleased to see me, even though I would, on occasions, be domineering and say disrespectful things to him – he took all the abuse I threw at him and never bore any ill feelings. My clothing reeked of moth repellent so I discarded it all completely, had a wash down in the kitchen whilst everyone was in the front room and donned some fresh clothing which had been laid out for me. Then I was ready to get back into my life.

The first port of call was Johnny Abbott's. When we arrived Scouse Eddie opened the door and he was looking really well. We covered as much ground as we could that day so that everyone knew I was back in circulation, which I think must have upset a few people. Come the evening we went to the Cable Street area and I collected some money off a restaurant owner in Commercial Road, then we went to The Mildmay in Newington Green where we met up with Reggie Kray again for a drink.

A few days after my release Ron and I were introduced to an official of the highways department of roadworks who was in charge of road works maintenance. This was the beginning of a venture which was quite legitimate, apart from the fact that we were obliged to give him a cash inducement.

In the Fifties central heating was practically unheard of in the London area and households would rely on an open fire for warmth in the winter months, so coal, coke or wooden logs were bought by the householder. The wooden tar blocks that had been laid down in many London streets were now being taken up and the streets resurfaced. These wooden blocks made good fuel for open fires but they were the property of the authorities who were doing the roadworks.

However, money talks and over a meal in a restaurant with the bent council official we came to a mutual agreement, shook hands on the deal and made arrangements to pay his asking price on the day they started to pull up the street, which was about a month away. This gave us plenty of time to organise ourselves. We acquired a yard in Wood Green in which to store the tar blocks and a lorry which we acquired pretty cheaply but on the understanding that we would return it if we found it unreliable.

We decided that we would need a labour staff of three, one to drive the lorry and two to fill the sacks and go on the knocker for prospective customers. I went to a cafe in Tottenham – Tom Miller's – where all the layabouts could be found and soon recruited the labour we needed.

On the first day of business we all turned up at the yard, picked up the lorry and went to the site. When we arrived they had already started digging up the road so I told them to start loading the lorry with the wooden tar blocks, take them back to the yard, unload them, then return to the site and collect another load. I met the council man as arranged and slipped him the money. He asked me if I was satisfied. I told him I would be if he got his workmen to load our lorry to save mine the trouble and he readily agreed, so it worked out fine as it left the other two guys to clean the blocks in the yard.

We arranged to pay them two pounds a day which was really good money in the days when the normal take home pay was about ten pounds basic for skilled workers for a 48-hour week. Of course we realised they would try to fiddle us so we worked out how many blocks it would take to fill a sack and how many sacks the lorry would hold. Then we told them we knew exactly how many tar blocks were loaded on to the lorry so we knew to the penny how much the takings would be.

I was at the yard at 8 a.m. the next day to see the lorry leave laden sky-high and down on the springs with the weight it was carrying. Fortunately it was an ex-army twin-wheel vehicle and could take the weight. At one o'clock Ron and I arrived with a pal at the Spaniard's in the Hampstead area, where they had been selling the blocks. At half past one the lorry arrived about half-laden. I sat with the driver in the front seats and he handed me the takings. A lot of it was in silver. The blocks were going well. Many of the householders had asked for our team to call back and others had asked for a card so that they could phone up. It looked as though we had stumbled on a legitimate and profitable game!

Back in the pub we unobtrusively counted out the money. It came to just over £60, which was a lot in those days, so we reckoned that after they had sold the remainder of the blocks that were left on the lorry we were looking at a load value of between £110 and £120. By the end of the day I had the rest of the money, which amounted to £52, and that meant that each load was fetching just over £115. The driver told me there were only about 20 tar blocks left on the lorry.

We realised we were on to a good thing but we also knew that our workers were basically layabouts and only worked spasmodically. We would have to safeguard ourselves by having fresh labour on hand and chopping and changing when necessary. We had full use of Bob's phone in the spieler which was handy for the incoming calls. One of our casual staff was a fella by the name of Sailor Barnes. He must have been about 40 years old and would tell the tallest, most unbelievable stories to impress anyone who would care to listen, especially the young teenagers. He was well known in the North London area, especially Stamford Hill where he would offer his services as a tree feller. It was all bravado – he never had a clue. On one occasion a Jewish woman made the mistake of getting him to chop a tree down on the cheap. Sailor made all the diagrams of where the tree would land and got to work with his axe. Finally the tree started to topple. Sailor shouted 'timber' as it was falling and it landed right bang on top of the next door neighbour's brand new outhouse.

The classic tall tale attributed to him was his stiff neck story. One day he was in Tom Miller's cafe when someone noticed his head was twisted to one side and he had difficulty moving his head to look straight ahead. He was asked what had happened and Sailor replied, 'What happened? I'll tell you what fucking happened. I was taking a load of gear up north and I was ten miles out of London on the A1 when all the forward gears went on the lorry and I had to drive the lorry all the way back home in reverse gear. That's what fucking happened.'

Sailor was alright in small doses, and handy for unskilled work. We only had him in the yard for a short while, for if by chance he saw the bonnet of the lorry up, in a matter of minutes he would have all the engine out and in bits and then do a disappearing act. We kept him well away from our lorry.

We had only been selling the tar blocks for a couple of weeks when we started getting complaints that the blocks had not been cleaned properly. When they were alight and burning in the fire grate the hot flames from the tar and wood would cause the small gritty stones to spit out all over the place. The problem was that when the wooden tar blocks were removed from the road the surface was covered with small particles of stone chippings, so to overcome this we put two extra-large steel water system tanks on concrete blocks, partly filled the tanks with water, made a fire under the tanks to heat the water and washed the tar blocks there. The small stones fell off with the aid of a scraper. A couple of disgruntled customers phoned the billiard hall to complain and Sailor picked the phone up. When the customers complained to him that the blocks were spitting stones at them Sailor replied, 'Well, spit back at them.' After that we realised he was bad news and he had to go, but we remained on good terms with him and would often give him a bit of silver if we bumped into him.

Unfortunately the winter was drawing to an end but we were still earning good money so we decided to keep the yard on, install some scales there, employ a trusted and tried friend as manager and buy in a bit of metal. This operation went well and soon we were running a regular scrap metal yard at Wood Green. We were still carrying out various other services of a dubious nature and the local police knew it, so Ron and I kept well in the background and the Old Bill never bothered us much.

We were making a good living out of tar blocks and looking after a few cafes and clubs, but were always on the lookout for other scams. We needed other ways to make money. The Krays were also trying to expand and looking at all sorts of opportunities. We often met with the twins and talked about ideas for business. Ronnie Kray's favourite was to be like the Messina brothers who for a number of years during the Forties and Fifties were the undisputed kings of organised vice in London. The Messinas bought vast amounts of properties in London to house the hookers they were bringing into England in hordes. They were known to have made a fortune and it was this that Ronnie Kray wanted to emulate. Part of the attraction was that Ronnie was a devout homosexual who loathed women so much that it would give him inner satisfaction to know he was living off hookers. When he talked about this his face would change and his eyes would bulge in the way they did when he was excited about something.

Ronnie actually sent one of his firm to Switzerland where the Messinas were hiding to negotiate setting up a new prostitution syndicate in London but the Krays were nicked before anything was done about it. There was also talk about setting up an organisation specialising in contract killings, like an English-style Mafia. Much of this Ronnie spoke to me about when we were on friendly terms and when his madness had temporarily lowered its ugly head. Whilst some of these suggestions were a bit rich for us, we couldn't spend the rest of our lives selling tar blocks, even though they were lucrative. We had to expand into other things. This was not too hard to do throughout the Fifties and early Sixties as hire purchase was in its infancy and credit freely available. Goods were practically forced on anyone on production of a cardboard rent book as proof of identity. The rent book could be purchased at practically any newsagent's for sixpence and, loaded with this and a few entries of bogus payments of rent, you could get quite a few things. I knew one firm in particular who would go to chemist's and barber's shops all over the country obtaining Remington electric shavers for 30 shillings deposit. The shop-keeper or barber wasn't concerned as the 30 shillings went straight into his pocket. This scam was operated on a big scale, as was the post office savings book fraud which was simplicity itself – all a firm needed was a child's John Bull printing outfit. All a person had to do was open savings account books at various accommoda-tion addresses with a pound or less in each. Then once the books arrived they would write in their own deposits, make a rubber stamp up, then draw the non-existent money that was never there in the first place at ten pounds a time daily at any post office. The withdrawals were limited to ten pounds but this scam could go on for a couple of weeks or more before it got dangerous, so a couple of hundred quid could be drawn out of each book – believe me, two hundred pounds was a lot of money in those days. But we decided not to bother too much with this particular money-earner

– it was too time-consuming and not really worthwhile, although many firms were beginning to make a lot of money from it. It seemed to us small-time with maybe plenty of bird in the offing.

We were by now spending a lot of time in the East End as we were minding and doing a lot of business with a couple of car dealers with premises in Mare Street. Cars could be bought with no deposit and many unscrupulous car dealers were boosting the price of the car up to cover a deposit. Some of the cars were complete wrecks but they were never inspected by the finance companies. Car sales sites were set up and hire purchase arranged with various finance companies. Customers were actually paid to buy and sign up for an old banger that had the price boosted sky-high. On many occasions we were paid money by the car dealers to take a car off their hands. All that was needed was an address where the documents could be sent. In most cases it would be a furnished room or even an accommodation address where mail could be forwarded and picked up.

One particular car dealer in Warren Street in the West End was buying late registered wrecks for literally next to nothing, boosting the purchase sky-high and paying us sometimes as much as £100 to get someone to sign up in a bogus name, though normally we would be getting between £20 and £30. This went on for a couple of years until the finance companies tightened up and started checking. By then they must have lost considerable amounts. Ironically, at a later date, we became repossession agents for Mercantile Credit and repossessed quite a number of cars and vans for them. I often wondered if any of the vehicles we repossessed for them we had been instrumental in acquiring for the customer in the first place. Flats and houses were acquired and goods bought on hire purchase. Even furnished rooms were filled up with goods on the HP. Sometimes the tenant would stay for three months until the letters arrived demanding payment. Even credit account betting was done.

I was seeing quite a lot of Tommy Smithson around this time. A friend of his told us all about a gambling device that was being used outside a number of London dog tracks. It was called a Spinning Jenny and was rigged with a hidden brake so that the mob running it could always win. I was quite impressed at the simplicity of its construction. After a few visits to various greyhound meetings with Smithson I soon learned all there was to know about the Spinning Jenny, which was to come in handy in the next couple of years.

Tommy Smithson and I worked many of the London dog tracks with the Spinning Jenny. It was a good earner. We would set up the board just before the last race. Of course we had no electric lights so our lighting came from candles in a jam jar. There were four or five in the team and normally it was a rigged game. One of us was the brake man who could stop the revolving arrow on a pinhead. The other member of our mob would act as punters and would watch where the mug punters placed their wager. When the arrow stopped spinning it would always be one or two of our men who were the winners.

At some London tracks we had an arrangement with the local constabulary to bring along someone to be nicked for gaming. It suited us and it suited the police as they could have a conviction. The man we brought along would get arrested for gaming, appear in court the following morning, plead guilty and get fined. We paid the fine and gave him a fiver for his trouble. That was a regular occurrence. As soon as we had set up the board I would be approached by a police constable and asked if we had brought a body along. On my affirmation we would commence the gaming. After a short while the PC would appear and say, 'OK, blow out the candles. You're nicked', and he would walk off with the body we had supplied. After they were out of sight we would relight the candles and recommence in earnest. It was just a case of supply and demand. This was an amicable arrangement with the Old Bill – the law was done and seen to be done.

Our man who did the spieling and worked the brake would start his line of patters as follows:

> 'OK folks, here we go!
> Round and round the arrow goes,
> Where it stops no one knows.
> Sometimes it's for thee,

Sometimes it's for me.
I'm young Johnny Fairplay,
All the way from Holloway,
Never known to run away.
You lay 'em and I'll pay 'em.
It's evens the reds,
Evens the whites,
Ten to one the heart,
And ten to one the jolly old diamond.'

He was really good at his job and could stop the arrow practically on a pinhead. After the last punter had left we would put our board in the trunk of the car and make our way to a nearby pub where we would count the spoils of our night's work.

Things ran smoothly enough although at some meetings as soon as we tried to set up the board it was confiscated, taken back to the nick and broken up so that we had to have another board made. But this caused no real problem as we knew a good carpenter who could knock one up in an hour or so. The only problem was the braking, but after 20 minutes of practice and an adjustment or two our brake man got it right.

After working the London dog tracks for so long we decided to work the track at Rye House outside London. We did really well there at the first couple of meetings, but after the fourth or fifth meeting, just as we had set up the board, about a dozen or so Old Bill pounced on us, some in uniform but most in plain clothes. They bundled us into a police van that was parked nearby and took us all to the local nick along with the board and trestle. After about half an hour or so they took us out of the cells and into a large room where we saw the board set up on the trestle.

There must have been about half a dozen Old Bill in the room looking really smug. Two of them were standing at the table facing each other, one where our brake man would stand and the other opposite him who would be used to steady the braking system. The one who seemed to be in charge was talking about fraud and obtaining money by deception and all manner of things. I could see what he was leading up to so I asked what he was talking about. At this he became all red in the face and said, 'That's a fucking crooked game you've got there.' I tried to play it down a bit and replied, 'How do you mean crooked?' He replied, 'The complete game is crooked. We know all about the device you have for stopping the arrow at whatever you want on the board.'

I knew we were in a bit of a tight spot and stalled him as best I could. I needed time to think. Suddenly I had the answer. 'No,' I replied. 'That device is just to slow the game down. If that wasn't there the arrow would spin for ages.' As diplomatically as possible I walked over to the board to spin the arrow and said, 'Can I show you what I mean?' By now he was fuming and replied, 'You fucking stay where you are. No, better still, get back in the cells.' We were all bundled unceremoniously back to the cells. After a couple of hours or so and a couple of phone calls, they unlocked the cells and beckoned us into a side room. They told us how despicable we were, showed us the door and warned us to steer well clear of their patch.

After all the aggravation we had at the flapping track at Rye House we decided just to work the London dog tracks that we were used to, although we were getting a bit fed up as the earnings were getting less. Because of this I came to the conclusion that one of our firm was on the fiddle, so I devised a plan to keep a check on the takings. I arranged that the three players on the Jenny must each empty a few boxes of matches into his pocket and every time a punter placed a pound stake, all our players were to take a match from one pocket and put it in the other pocket, and for every ten shillings that a punter wagered a matchstick was to be broken in half and put in the other pocket. This would at least take care of the notes, as at the end of the play we would all go to the local pub where a roll call would be made of all the whole matches and half matches. We weren't too worried about the silver as no one was going to be foolish enough to risk a rub down for undeclared silver. Most of the time the count would tally.

I remember one incident when I thought I would be off to Durham Fair where most of the gangs would go once a year in the summer months. We always had a good time at Durham Fair and always earned well with the Spinning Jenny. Durham Fair was like a busman's holiday for us but we were always pleased to get back to London even though I knew Ron would be looking after things properly. I remember Scarface Jimmy Spinks and his firm would go there, with Spinksy sitting in a big armchair on the back of an open truck.

By now we were friendly enough with Roger the car dealer who had a car site at Clapton (near Stamford Hill) and another car showroom at Finchley. Occasionally he would ask us to supply a bit of muscle which we willingly did for a fee. Roger was selling cars with private HP deals and would have problems with non-payments. We would go to the purchaser's house and sit outside till he drove off in his car. We would follow him and when he arrived wherever he was going, it was easy enough to threaten him – he would usually hand over any cash he had for arrears without a struggle. As well as paying us, Roger also supplied us with a couple of decent cars and the services of his mechanic free of charge should a car be in need of a repair.

CHAPTER EIGHT

Protection

The Kray firm was developing. They were learning whom they could frighten and how to gain from it. Their reputation was growing and they were sticking their fingers in every pie they could. Mulla, a bully, but terrified of cold steel, had teamed up with the Kray twins. They toured parts of London in a Sunbeam Talbot car calling on thieves who they knew had stolen a lorryload of goods. It was the Krays' hangers-on and the boys that Ronnie bedded that kept them informed of what was happening. The Krays would assure the thieves that they had a buyer who wouldn't ask any questions. Then they'd hijack the load and the thieves could do nothing. Soon thieves and villains were afraid to admit to the Krays that they'd done a scam or robbery and they'd speak in whispers in case the Krays got to know of it. If, for instance, the Krays got to know that a thief had just acquired a lorryload of goods they would arrive with members of their gang in another lorry and just help themselves.

If a thief stood his ground one of the Krays would say: 'Well, it's up to you. You either take a drink off us or we'll get on the blower and you're nicked.' By this they meant, 'You sell us the goods for next to nothing or we'll telephone the police.' Fences were also the prey of the Krays and when they were relieved of their stolen property on a promise, there was nothing they could do about it.

The twins knew everything that was happening in their manor. No one could do anything without them knowing – they had a grapevine second to none. Everyone wanted to be in their good books so everything that happened was reported back to them. Even if you were just having a friendly drink with one of them he'd say, 'You was with so-and-so last night', or 'We've heard you did such-and-such a thing'. A lot of this information came from young guys who scurried back to Ronnie with everything they heard. Every one of them had been bedded by Ronnie and each was anxious to be his number one lover and be fawned on by him and taken out to a pub or for a meal. It never occurred to Ronnie's young morons that Ronnie changed his bed-mates, lovers or sex slaves like he changed his shirts. Even today there are Kray scum visiting Broadmoor with their little bits of news and Ronnie knows what's going on in the criminal world. Fortunately he can no longer relieve thieves of their goods, but he knows who is where and what they are all doing.

Tony Mulla ended in the pornography racket and then in the late Fifties he and Alfie Melvin took over a number of new strip clubs in Soho and got very rich. In 1959 or 1960, when they were at their best in the strip club game, they quarrelled. Melvin shot Tony dead then shot himself.

But at this time we were doing OK and never needed the Krays. We were also looking after a few restaurants and clubs. Our outfit was growing stronger in numbers, although The Bear allowed himself to be swayed by the Krays into becoming a member of their firm, even though we were all doing well. At first he was only superficially involved with the Krays but in the years that were to come he served a couple of prison sentences due to the Krays involving him and using him.

A lot of people call protection 'the protection racket' but it's no more a racket that many other businesses. They think it's a violent way to make money, but in fact it prevents a lot of violence because it stops the really unruly mobs from breaking the law when and how they want. Pubs, cafes, clubs, spielers, amusement arcades and some restaurants are places that need protection of some sort or other, otherwise they couldn't stay in business. They are places that attract liberty-takers and weekend gangsters, who have a few drinks then go into these places and smash them up. Snooker halls always need protection because the baize on the tables can get easily torn, and in amusement arcades just one machine getting broken can be expensive. The owners of these places wanted our protection. It was for their own safety and guaranteed they could stay in business.

Sometimes they had to be reminded that they needed protection and normally this was done by getting another firm to visit the target and cause as much aggravation as possible so as to cause a drop in the target's trade. If there was a doorman or a bouncer, he would be beaten senseless. At no time was protection mentioned. The important thing was that if an establishment got a bad name it would be closed down. The owner knew this, so was not liable to call the police. Illegal establishments were particularly vulnerable.

After the aggravation was completed, the next step was to approach the owner, who knew you or knew of you, and tell him you heard he was having problems and you could make his headaches disappear. It was suprising how they took the bait, especially an unlicensed spieler or a clip joint. Then when you had settled accounts with the firm who had caused the aggro for you, they would come to the drinking club or restaurant and you would tell the owner that these two or three guys had joined your firm. In this way you gave the other firm perks, for they could now use the premises free of charge. The proprietor was happy to stand this because the violence had stopped.

A firm like mine offered a good deal to the owners. In some areas this was the only way to have law and order. Sometimes if the owner wasn't paying for protection his business might get burgled or another firm would start trouble and smash his place up. If we didn't get the fee, some other firm would. To have a regular arrangement with a well-known person they could trust saved them money. We were offering a real service, unlike other people who would just steam in demanding money with menaces. When this happened, we'd be waiting for them the next time they came. If the local tearaways knew that a club or pub was being protected by a firm like ours they behaved themselves.

Usually there were two kinds of payments. One was for off-licences and pubs and small shops where we could carry away a case or two of booze. This was cheap for protecting a shop in a rough area. The other payment was for restaurants, spielers and cafes who would willingly pay a weekly sum to guarantee them peaceful trading.

Soon we found ourselves looking after many clubs, spielers restaurants and places in Harringay, Wood Green, Stoke Newington and Stamford Hill. Some of these people approached us – more so the illegal drinking clubs and spielers who could ill afford to draw attention to themselves. They had to have a trouble-free ride and we were their insurance. People were also coming to us with different schemes and ideas. Others just came to us because they had had a bit of aggravation from someone and wanted us to settle the score for a price. In most cases we readily agreed.

In 1956 a good friend of mine, Bobby Ramsey, the boxer, was in a bit of trouble that involved the Krays and later involved me. I had first met Bobby Ramsey when I was a deserter from the army. He was a bit of a character who always dressed very sharp in a black coat and pigskin gloves. He came out of Hoxton and was a friend of my cousin, Chrissy Hawkins, and Punchy Hines, who was married to cousin Chrissy's sister Patsy. Bobby Ramsey was at one time the right-hand man of Billy Hill who was 'King of London's Underworld' until Billy retired. I had always got on well with Ramsey and had a lot of respect for him then as I have today. I still see quite a lot of him. He's in his mid-sixties now but he is still minding a pub in East London.

The trouble started when we heard that Ronnie Kray had been nicked with Bobby Ramsey for causing GBH (grievous bodily harm) or some similar charge to a docker called Terry Martin who had inadvertently got mixed up with one of the Kray firm wars. I later learned that Bobby was alleged to have stabbed Terry Martin with a bayonet. After he and Ronnie Kray had fled the scene their car had been stopped by the police. They found the blood-covered bayonet in the car and a gun on Ronnie Kray. It was loaded with dum-dum bullets which do not just make a hole in a person but tear a great gaping wound.

Shortly after Bobby and Ronnie Kray were nicked I was approached by Reggie Kray whilst I was having a quiet drink in a pub called the Three Crowns which I used in Stoke Newington. Reggie did not know my companions enough to confide in them so he asked me if he could have a word with me in private.

I left my friends and joined Reggie at a small table out of earshot from his companions and mine. He started the conversation by saying that I probably knew that his Ronnie had been nicked. I told him I was aware of the situation. He then went on to say that the guy, Terry Martin, who had taken the beating could not be bribed or got at and his brother was looking at a lot of bird. Seeing as I was off the manor and unknown to Terry Martin I could fit him up and discredit him as a witness against Reggie's brother. I thought about the situation and all the possibilities and told him I would have to involve other people who would insist on some money up front. He readily agreed. No price was fixed at that moment but I did warn him that what he was asking wouldn't come cheap. I arranged to try and sort something out within the next couple of days. He suggested I meet him again at his mother's home but I was against this for safety reasons and suggested we meet at the Three Crowns again in two days. Again he agreed. We left it at that and returned to our own companions.

At the time I had every intention of fitting up Martin as I had no time for villains who grassed on other villains because things went wrong, but at the same time there was no way I would put myself out on a limb for Ronnie Kray. I didn't really need Kray money but in any event I would make sure I got my dues before I got Ronnie Kray off the hook – the Krays had a bad track record when it came to settling their accounts. I made a mental note of all the relevant things I would need to ask and know about Martin's drinking habits and so on but in the meantime our own livelihood was of paramount importance – the Kray matter would have to wait until we drew some money off Reggie before we would even consider getting involved. I put it out of my mind until the meeting that we had arranged.

On the day of the meeting Reggie was there before me and my brother Ron. Reggie was with two pals whom he left to join us at the bar. I told him we had devised a plan but before the plan was to be put into operation we would want full and final settlement. In the meantime we would expect a few hundred pounds for expenses as other people would be involved and, seeing as I had no idea what Terry Martin looked like, a description of him and details of the haunts he frequented would be essential. He furnished me with the information and handed me an envelope which contained £300, which was quite a considerable sum of money in those days. I made it clear that the £300 we had received was for any expenses we would incur in setting this thing up.

The plan was to fit Terry Martin up with a rape charge. I knew a woman whom I could trust implicitly to go along with us all the way. She was one hundred per cent reliable and most of all could stand up to the strain of any police probe and interrogation to which she would be subjected.

Reggie was elated at the plan and gave me the names of a couple of pubs where Martin might be drinking. But any plans of an initial meeting between Martin and the woman conspirator, at a place known to be frequented by Martin, were sure to be disastrous. The police would be sure to smell a rat if a woman came to them with the story that she'd gone into a strange pub, on her own, in a strange neighbourhood, then walked off with a complete stranger to some unknown destination and screamed rape. No one would buy this from her, so obviously the initial meeting would have to be better than the crude suggestions of Reggie Kray. And much more money would be required up front in cash as soon as the phoney rape was reported.

We did intend to honour our agreement and the following evening we were in Stepney searching out Terry Martin – without success. But in the meantime we learned that all was not as it seemed and that Terry Martin was an innocent victim who was in the wrong place at the wrong time and took a terrible beating in lieu of his older brother. Martin didn't stand a chance against his assailants – he was slashed with a bayonet and given a good kicking and could easily have died. So we dropped it and did not pursue the matter any further and considered the £300 as expenses for the time and effort we had put into the matter. If I had known at the time the full set of circumstances I wouldn't have gone along with the plot, nor would Ronnie or any of our firm, and I feel now that Reggie should have done something about it personally. So we forgot all about it and waited to see if there were any repercussions.

Soon it was all over the place that we had turned the twins over but we did not see it this way as we thought we had been misled. At the time Ron and I were living in a flat we had at North Grove, South Tottenham. I heard Reggie was making all kinds of threats but I never took much notice as even he must have realised no one in their right mind could or would get involved. We were by now getting deeply involved with Roger the car dealer but he was making a lot of enemies because he had a bit of backing. We did not mind sorting out his problems as he was free with his money and he had recently given me a bright yellow Cadillac as a gift.

The end of all this was that Ronnie Kray was jailed for three years for the GBH charge and also for being in possession of a loaded revolver. Ramsey got seven years reduced to five on appeal. Reggie was found not guilty. Everyone was pleased when Ronnie was put away and although the Kray firm went on operating, fewer innocent people were attacked for no apparent reason. By now Ronnie Kray was so paranoid that you couldn't look sideways at him without risking a beating. He nearly killed a Berwick Street doorman just for referring to them as 'the boys'. And at the Old Horns public house Ronnie gouged a man in the face with a pint glass just for staring him straight in the eye. This to Ronnie was a challenge, and as long as he had his backing along he would rise to it with viciousness. He once nearly killed a guy at a party because the guy threw Ronnie's coat on the floor. And another guy who said, 'You're putting on a bit of weight, Ron', had his face cut to ribbons. Every time he looks in the mirror he is reminded of that encounter – he had to have 72 stitches.

Some time after Ronnie was convicted a drinking club owned by the Martin family in Poplar was set alight. Everyone was sure that this was a vengeance attack, but Reggie had a watertight alibi. He was fishing with a policeman friend in Suffolk.

Shortly after Ronnie and Bobby Ramsey were jailed I heard that some strangers were making enquiries as to where I was living. A bit later I was alone and fast asleep in our flat, which was on the first floor of a private house in North Grove when, in the early hours of the morning, the door was kicked off and I was confronted by four fellas all armed and lashing out at me with coshes and knives. Fortunately I had taken the precaution of concealing a long-bladed knife under my pillow but the odds were so overwhelming I was fighting a losing battle. I managed to stay on my feet and keep from being knocked unconscious. I managed to cut at least one of them but finally finished up needing over 70 stitches in my face and several more in head wounds, along with the bumps and bruises. Some time later I was to meet one of my assailants when he had no back-up and the odds were reversed.

It would have been much worse had I not had my back to the wall or had I lost consciousness and slumped to the floor under the hail of blows that were rained at my head. I kept my feet and managed to drive to the hospital where I was stitched up and X-rayed. I had no broken bones. The duty doctor wanted to keep me in hospital overnight for observation but I resisted and got in my car and drove home. I was in a bit of a mess so I never moved out of the flat for almost a week. When all the bruising had gone down and the skin had knitted together I was able to take the stitches out myself with the aid of a small pair of scissors, some tweezers and some TCP to avoid infection. My brother Ron was fuming when he found out what had happened but he realised you have to take these things lying down and there was no way of getting back at the twins as they were always surrounded by minders and never alone.

As can be expected I had the usual bombardment from the lunatic fringe expressing their wishes to join me in a revenge attack but I knew it was just bravado talk in an effort to maybe endear themselves to me. So I told them politely that we would take care of things when the time was right. It was hard not to be rude to these people who were ordinary working folk without the slightest idea of the kind of world I was part of, no more than I could understand their orderly world.

A few years later I became friendly with Buller Ward, who had also been cut badly by Reggie Kray. He was full of hate for the twins and would come to me with various plans to get rid of the Krays permanently. And we were not the only ones seeking revenge.

CHAPTER NINE

'An Opportunist's Dream'

We'd been running the Spinning Jenny less and less and it was dying a slow death. In the beginning we had found it all amusing but now that our suspicions had been aroused that someone was cheating us we got a bit fed up and we gradually began to phase it out. We had never worked the Jenny for the money for we were doing well looking after a number of cafes and clubs in Cable Street. We were also looking after the Lancaster snooker club and Johnny Abbott's spieler and minding several restaurants in Green Lanes in Harringay. However the Spinning Jenny had been quite lucrative while it lasted and we had a lot of laughs.

I was seeing a lot of Tommy Smithson and would spend time with him in his spieler in Soho. I've always had a great regard for Smithson as a man who had such courage – I don't think he knew the word fear. Many times I've known him to be cut and have his face slashed to ribbons but as soon as the wounds would heal he would be back to settle the score. I often suggested he join up with us as there was practically no risk and we had some good connections, but he wouldn't budge. He said he was happy as he was. I always felt a bit sad whenever I left him. He was deeply devoted to his girlfriend Faye and maybe he felt he would have to uproot himself. But whatever his reasons he was adamant.

We continued our deal with the bent public highway official and still stored the wooden tar blocks in the Wood Green yard as it was pretty legitimate and lucrative. What's more it was highly organised, as come the winter we had two door-to-door salesmen who would canvass the various areas on a commission-only basis, any commission to be paid after delivery of the order. At this particular time we found out we were having some scrap copper pilfered from the yard during the night so we installed a couple of dogs to look after things.

All through 1954 we became good pals with a fella called Dickie Swash, usually called Dixie, one of a family of five brothers. At the time he was living at home with his family in Lorenco Road (nicknamed Little Russia) and we would spend a lot of time there. During the summer months the residents would sit on the steps outside their houses talking and passing the time of day. At this time hire-purchase, Provident and tally men were running rampant throughout London and you could be sure that if a tally man arrived in Little Russia with a large van laden with goods, every resident in Lorenco Road would have two of everything on board the van. Within an hour the van would be empty and the tally man would drive off well pleased. Unbeknown to him all the customers had used fictitious names.

It was only when the tally man called for his weekly payment that the penny dropped. The residents had everything and everyone from carpet salesmen to vacuum cleaner salesmen. At the finish things got so bad that the entire road was blacklisted nationwide. I was told by a reliable source that one unlucky salesman who was unaware of the blacklist on Lorenco Road sold the entire contents of his van and when he went back to his firm with all the fictitious names they could not believe he had sold goods in good faith – he nearly ended up in court on criminal charges.

The mid-Fifties was an opportunist's dream and we were into everything. It was about this time I met Billy Welsh again, one of The Bear's several brothers. We got on really well and in many ways his outlook on life was very similar to Tommy Smithson in his unpretentious and non-caring attitude. For some reason Billy and his brother The Bear would often be rowing and at war with each other and to this day I have no idea why there was sometimes so much hostility between them. Over the years I became really close to Billy and his wife Isabelle. When their marriage broke up Billy and his three children Joey, Bill and Emma moved in with me and my family. I honestly could not fault the man and all the years we spent together we never had one cross word and never ever cheated one another out of a penny. He was almost as big as The Bear and had a lot of courage. I remember one day we were both in a pub called The Favourite at Hornsey Rise when all of a sudden a fella called Andrews pulled a tool on him and cut Billy on the neck. It wasn't much of a cut and I don't think he realised he had been cut, but he turned around and smashed his fist straight in Andrews' face. I was watching Billy's back to make sure nobody jumped him from behind but nobody did. Within seconds it was all over and we walked out of the pub where there was a costermonger's barrow that was laden with fruit. Billy suddenly upended the cart, sending all the fruit and veg rolling down Hornsey Rise (The Favourite is on a hill). It was funny to see all the apples, oranges and potatoes careering down the hill. I said to him, 'What did you do that for?' and he replied, 'Because it's Andrews' fucking barrer.'

Although I knew him from my days as a deserter it was not until 1955 that I had any business deals with him. The cold war between him and his brother, The Bear, went on. But blood is thicker than water, so in a way, because Billy was on my firm and The Bear was on the Krays' firm, that was a bit of extra insurance between me and the Krays.

I was spending a lot of time at Johnny Abbott's spieler – he had been getting a bit worried about all the attention he was getting. He thought he was attracting the wrong clientele as a little mob from Wood Green had recently started frequenting the house and taking liberties. I thought he was making a mountain out of a molehill and maybe getting a bit paranoid, but I sorted the Wood Green mob out for him. Johnny was basically a straight person and I think that maybe the pressure of running a spieler was getting to him. But whilst I was there, there were no problems except for the occasional drunk whom I would sling out. But, as I explained to him, every gambling or drinking establishment gets this aggravation.

We were using several pubs and restaurants for meetings and deals. One of these was The Mildmay Tavern where we often had a drink with the Krays. Around this time I was letting a young kid about 17 years old called Roy sleep in the office in the scrapyard at Wood Green – he was unhappy at home as he did not get on with his mother and stepfather. Understanding his problem, it was natural for me to feel compassionate. One particular evening we were in The Mildmay Tavern about four-handed and we had brought the young boy along with us. We had been in there about 20 minutes when the Kray twins came in with a couple of guys. We said our hellos and they joined us in a drink. As soon as he saw young Roy, Ronnie Kray could not take his eyes off him. I noticed the boy was getting a bit worried at all the attention he was getting. Up until now he had never met Ronnie Kray and had no idea he was homosexual. He became alarmed and confused at the way Ronnie Kray came to sit next to him and whispered to him. Like me, my brother had noticed all the interest being showered on the young kid so he decided to take the initiative by saying, 'Come on, it's time we moved on', and we all rose from our seats and said our goodbyes.

I noticed how peeved Ronnie Kray became when he saw us leaving. None of us mentioned the incident when we got back in the car but I realised it had not gone unnoticed – Ronnie Kray was not very subtle in anything he did. Not wanting to embarrass the boy in front of the others, I waited for an opportune time to ask him what Ronnie Kray was talking to him about so secretively. It turned out that Ronnie Kray had asked the boy if he would like to go to a party they were on their way to that night and then went on to say that after the party the boy could spend the night with him. Obviously the kid became quite alarmed at this outright statement and said words to the effect that he wasn't that sort of person – Ronnie Kray kept on insisting by saying, 'Come on, you might like it.' I felt sorry for the kid as he was a naive boy and I would hate to think of him falling into the hands of Ronnie Kray. I knew from past experience of seeing him chat up young boys how persistent he would be and how he would make a fuss of them and cater for their every whim. He really thought that because he himself was that way inclined all young boys would be likewise. It never entered his head that a boy could have ideas different to his.

Around this time Ron and I were hearing constantly about an up and coming, non-caring, non-fearing young fella aged about 18 named John May and nicknamed 'Chang'. We first met Chang some years ago when he was aged about 15, when we would frequent Lorenco Road where he was living with his parents. Now we were also seeing him at the Salt Beef Bar at Stamford Hill and Johnny Stock's all-night cafe. It was apparent even from those early days that he would become a key figure in our organisation. He thought along the same lines as us and was very streetwise but sometimes he could be a bit of a hothead.

He had just finished a stint in some young offenders' institute. He was unemployed and just getting bored with his lot. He seemed very much older in his appearance and attitude than he actually was. Soon we began to hear quite a lot about his escapades and battles, all of which were against hardened men known for their fighting prowess, not mugs or weekend villains. He already had six convictions.

On a couple of occasions that I was in front of the magistrates for something or other Chang was there also on some assault charge or other. Even at this early age he was quite ruthless and fearless. On one occasion he set about a couple of brothers who had come to his home to sort him out and he finished up chasing them up the road with a butcher's meat cleaver. He joined us in the end and was very loyal. He got to really hate both the Kray twins.

For the next week or so Chang was with us day and night and got on well with everyone he met. He seemed a far cry from the young rebellious teenager Ron and I had met a few years back. Now his manner and attitude was that of a self-assured young man in his twenties who could be quite charming when he wanted to be.

By this time our scrapyard in Wood Green was busy trading legitimately but we were not averse to dealing with the occasional dubious load of metal from people we trusted. The size of the fee paid depended on the load. As can be imagined this was quite risky so it was not a facility available to just anybody, but seeing as it was lucrative we would usually be obliging to people we could trust.

I thought Chang would be interested in running the yard as every other household in Lorenco Road was an amateur scrap iron merchants – they would literally dismantle cars in the road outside their front door. When the vehicle had been picked dry of spare parts and was resting on bricks, the carcass would be manhandled on to a lorry and carted off to a scrap iron yard – but not our yard as our premises were not large enough to cater for scrap iron and we only dealt in scrap metal.

A few days after Chang joined our firm we realised he was bored with the scrap metal side of our business and was more interested in the protection. So we readily agreed to let him in on that side as he was an exceptional person with all the right credentials. He had proved his loyalty many times and was trusted implicitly. We knew that if he was pulled in by the Old Bill he would deny anything and everything. Also he was fearless and if you were fighting side by side, he would go on till he dropped.

One lunchtime Chang and I were in a pub in Harringay where we had just done a deal with a couple of guys. We were about to leave when a couple of Scouse fellas walked in. Chang was at the bar and I was sitting at the table. I was facing the door with my back towards Chang. Suddenly I turned round to see the two men setting about Chang. I rushed over, picked up a large glass ashtray from a table and smashed it with all my might against one of their heads. The other was kneeling over Chang. His head was at my waist level and I kicked him full in the face. I had to flee the scene quickly as there was a warrant out for my arrest at the time. We piled in the car and fled. For weeks after Chang showed his determination by practically living in the pub hoping they would return so that he could sort them out.

Although by now we had given up the Spinning Jenny, Chang

had heard so much about the crooked wheel that he was anxious to see how it operated. I told him we had bled it dry and most of the punters who frequented the dog tracks were wise to the rigged game and those who weren't were educated by those who were. I thought that we were finished with the Jenny but then someone suggested we set up a game in Petticoat Lane on Sundays as it was packed with people, many of whom were tourists. Money was in abundance then, but we were always on the lookout for other little earners so we decided to get the wheel out again.

Petticoat Lane is under the jurisdiction of the City of London Police, who are considered the élite of the Metropolitan Police, and we thought it unlikely that they would make a major issue out of street gaming. At worst we would be moved on if we had come to their attention and then we could go and plot up somewhere else and resume the play. After some thought we agreed it would be a good way to spend a few hours on a Sunday and that we might go and snatch a couple of hundred. A date for the venture into new territory was set for the following Sunday.

On Sunday morning we all met – that is my brother Ron, myself, Billy Welsh, Chang and Percy Smith, who was to be the brake man and do the spieling. Chang already knew all there was to know about gaming. We all piled into my yellow Cadillac, put the gaming board in the boot and arrived at Petticoat Lane around half past eight, just as it started getting busy. We parked the car and set the board up on a bombed site off Middlesex Street. The piece of ground where we were was a bit higher than the surrounding area, which gave us a vantage point for spotting the Old Bill. Also in our favour was that the City of London Police are much taller than the Metropolitan Police and so could be spotted a mile off.

We seemed to be getting a lot of hostile looks from some stallholders but we had quite a long spell without interruptions and packed up around lunchtime. We had done better than was expected and finished up clearing just over £300. Of course we had used the match tally system again but once again the tally didn't check out, so we came to the conclusion that someone had difficulty in keeping count.

Chang thought it was all a bit exciting and we decided to give it another go the following week. But the Old Bill must have been waiting for us. Before we even had time to set the game up, half-a-dozen burly coppers pounced on us and bundled us into a police van. I learned later from the senior officer that the previous Sunday after the market several stallholders had lodged complaints about us and justice had to be seen to be done.

In a very short space of time we were all in the City of London nick – as well as an innocent bystander whom the Old Bill had rounded up thinking he was part of the team. He was going frantic protesting his innocence and imploring me to tell them that he was nothing to do with us. We thought it was really amusing and kept insisting to him that we were just innocent victims like him. After a time the situation was getting really hilarious and he honestly didn't know whether he was coming or going. By now he was thinking in terms of what his punishment would be. I remember Billy Welsh telling him that if he had never been nicked for gaming before he was probably looking at about three months. At this stage it was hard keeping a straight face. Finally a senior officer came into the interview room where we were being held (after being let out of the cells) accompanied by two of the biggest Old Bill I'd ever seen. Both of them were bigger than The Bear.

I think the Old Bill were now aware of the situation with the straight guy and saw the funny side too as they were probably listening outside the door. They apologised and told him he could go. The officer in charge showed no animosity to us, which I found confusing. He told me almost apologetically that he would have to confiscate the board. The City of London were definitely a cut above the Metropolitan Police – a different breed entirely. Naturally he gave us a warning to keep off the City manor. I then got talking to the two huge Old Bill. They seemed to have a wicked but likeable sense of humour when we spoke about the innocent bystander who got involved. I gathered that even though they were ordinary police constables their IQs must be much higher than those of their counterparts in the Metropolitan force so I assumed that they must sit a much stiffer test than their comrades.

I was the last to leave the City of London Police Station after receiving the by now proverbial lecture which, I suppose, they were duty bound to give. Within a few minutes I had joined Ron and the rest outside the nick. The innocent guy had long gone. I suppose after checking us out with the CRO (Criminal Records Office) they realised he was not connected with us. We had lost our board but although we had a spare one in the office of the yard, we decided we had finally bled the Spinning Jenny dry.

In 1956 Jack Spot retired and Billy Hill ('King of the Underworld') went off to live in Spain. Their time was over and the rackets were there for the taking. The year 1956 was also when the Suez Crisis erupted and petrol went on ration and became scarce. I hit on the idea of turning this crisis to our advantage and earning a bit of money. All the taxi cab drivers were feeling the pinch and their cabs which were then running on petrol, not diesel, were standing idle. You could ask practically anything for petrol.

We still had the ex-army lorry we used for carting scrap metal and I knew where I could get plenty of 40-gallon steel drums. All we needed to do was fill them up with water and float a gallon or so of petrol on top, replace the stopper, load them on the lorry and bingo – the customers were practically begging for it. The greedy ones would want two or three, so we obliged. Mind you, we couldn't work the same area two days running but London's a big place and we always found plenty of customers, especially amongst the taxi cabs. Of course we had a lot of rucks but we always maintained we bought the drums of petrol in good faith.

By this time Ron and I had got fed up with all the aggravation I was getting over the tar blocks, so we put a manager in the yard to run things, which suited us better. I heard all about the Krays' activities and knew they were sniffing around the Tottenham area with Tony Mulla. I heard from a reliable source that along with Mulla they were looking for an easy mark to mug off as Mulla had asked a friend of mine if he knew of a thief who had scored, or a fence whom they could put the blag on, or maybe a fence who had recently bought some bent gear that they could steam into and ease him out of. But they drew a blank and drove off in Mulla's Sunbeam Talbot looking elsewhere.

I would often see Tony Mulla's car parked outside Shelley and Pepsi's Restaurant in the High Road, Tottenham, and learned that Pepsi was making a book. Mulla, knowing this, kept phoning bets through. He was running up a big gambling debt which Pepsi had no chance of recovering, so he eventually shut shop with regards to the bookmaking business. It peeved Mulla that I had no time for him. He wasn't involved in much and was always scratching around and looking to get into something, but I wasn't going to educate him. It really used to wind him up when I would park my yellow Cadillac Coupe de Ville directly near his little Sunbeam Talbot. I think in those years we just tolerated each other and he could not push his luck with me as it was well known that I always carried a tool or always had one close at hand. Vain person that he was, he could not stand the thought of being cut.

Around this time the Kray twins were going about being violent for violence's sake. Every week I would hear of someone somewhere taking a beating by the Krays and their firm. Again they were showing a complete lack of imagination in their exploits, being able only to take the fruits of other people's work by threatening them with a beating. They were beginning to build up their protection racket. They were not too clever at it at first and Reggie Kray was jailed for 18 months for demanding money with menaces from the owner of a leather shop in Hampstead. He made the elementary mistake of doing both the demanding and the damage himself. With Ronnie left in command while his twin was in Wandsworth the firm's business went downhill. As usual, all Ronnie was interested in were his private wars.

Years later they were still making the same kind of mistakes. In 1965 they were nicked for demanding money with menaces. They made various appeals and went as far as possible to obtain bail but the filth strongly opposed it and they remained in custody. Finally they got Lord Boothby to speak up for them in the House of Lords and he was told to shut up and sit down as the Kray matter did not concern them – or words to that effect. During their couple of months in Brixton on remand they got a private detective named Devlin to check up on their accuser who was the son of a baronet who was tainted and rumoured to be a homosexual. Finally they were acquitted. Due to all the dignitaries, nobility and top bull pigs being involved, a hands off the Krays message was sent out and they were practically given a licence to do what they wanted. This was the reason the Old Bill set up a special unit in Tintagel House.

At that time there was a sexual relationship going on between Ronnie Kray and Lord Boothby. I don't know who was having who. I don't think anyone knew although George Cornell reckoned they were sharing young boys and later on Boothby was being blackmailed as he had unwisely put his trust in Ronnie Kray. Gay parties were often held in Ronnie Kray's flat in Cedra Court, Cazenove Road, Stamford Hill (not Walthamstow as recently reported), and at the Glenrae Hotel, Seven Sisters Road, Finsbury Park. Boothby was not the only politician to frequent the parties. There was also Tom Driberg, a homosexual MP, and a couple of high-ranking police officers. One of the pigs was attached to the vice squad, and even men of the cloth (priests) were known to frequent the parties, plus a sprinkling of young boys of all colours and creeds.

The Krays treated members of their firm like errand boys. They had to obey every order immediately. They took the twins' washing to the laundry and did all their shopping. When they were good they got presents but when they were bad they got a beating. To make themselves look good the twins would call a meeting of the firm if anyone in the underworld got nicked and then make a collection for them. If the collection raised £100, then £80 would go in the twins' pockets.

Also about this period Billy Welsh developed a bad heart condition and became the first man to have open heart surgery on TV. He was an extremely genial man and when asked, as he often was, about his heart operation, he would jokingly say his heart was too big (meaning he was too big-hearted and generous) so they had to cut part of it away.

One day we had arranged to meet Punchy Hines in the Old Basin House, Shoreditch, on the borders of Bethnal Green. I was accompanied by my brother Ron, Billy Welsh and Chang. We had just ordered our drinks when I looked in the mirror behind the bar and spotted Harry Sullivan, who was one of the four who cut me that night in my flat after the Terry Martin affair. He had not yet noticed me. I quickly told Ron and the others who he was and Ron wanted to set about him there and then. But I told Chang to go out to the car and fetch the knife that was under the driving seat. Within seconds Chang was back and by this time Harry Sullivan had noticed me and all the colour had drained from his face.

Ironically there was four of us, just like there were four of them when they cut me up badly. I had waited for this moment for a long time. I couldn't take my eyes off him and he was looking from one of us to the other, not knowing what to do. After what must have seemed an eternity for him I walked up to him. Ron followed me and Chang and Billy Welsh stood at the door in case he decided to make a run for it. When I stood next to him I asked him where his pals were today. He mumbled something or other and started grovelling, so I cut him there and then where he stood and left him in a heap on the floor. We all got out of there pretty quickly in case someone had called the law. To this day I do not know what he was mumbling about nor have I heard or seen him or his three pals since. They seemed to have vanished off the face of the earth.

By now we had heard that The Bear was seeing a lot of the Krays who were enticing him on to their firm. I don't think Billy Welsh was too pleased at the news as by now the Krays were taking a lot of liberties. Even though a couple of months had elapsed since I had become aware of Billy's anger over something that went on between him and his brother The Bear, he was still insistent on seeing The Bear, so the two of us decided on driving over to the snooker hall that the Krays were running in Mile End. It was a pretty warm day and as we drove on to the vacant piece of land outside the snooker club, both the twins were outside with two of their sidekicks getting a bit of fresh air. By now Billy was in a bit of a rage so God alone knows what went on between him and The Bear.

When we had parked the car we walked towards the Krays who stood their ground. When we were in front of them Billy asked them if they knew where Tommy was, to which they replied,

'No.' Billy then went on to say, 'Well, if you fucking well knew you wouldn't tell, would you?' God knows what was going through their minds as he unleashed this effrontery at them. I was expecting all hell to break loose, but the next thing Billy turned away and we walked back to the car. When we were getting in I noticed Ronnie Kray dash back into the snooker hall. As we were driving away I noticed that several more of their mob had come outside the club.

Again I realised the Krays were not so invulnerable as everyone seemed to think, and their strength was in the huge following they had. I was a bit surprised that Reggie never made reference to the £300 I had off him and I never bothered explaining to him how I felt about the plot with Terry Martin. As we were driving along Billy said to me, 'I don't know why Tom is getting involved with them. They're only using him and he'll finish up doing a lot of bird down to them. The pair of them haven't got any bottle.'

I think by now what grievances he had with regards to The Bear were diminishing. We decided to drive over to Stamford Hill and have a salt beef sandwich in the E & A, with a feller called Dave Clare who came from Walthamstow. He was a big, dark-haired, good-looking guy who had been having a lot of trouble with Eric the Horse, one of the local villains who ran Walthamstow. Eric was of German origin and his real name was Ernest Horste. He was a big fella and a loner who once broke a woman's arm in a pub. On one occasion we were in Walthamstow market where Dave Clare's mother had a stall, and the Horse went up to another stall and demanded money. When the stallholder refused the Horse walked into a nearby hardware shop, got hold of a butcher's knife, went back to the stall, chopped the stallholder right across the hand and severed one of his fingers. Anyhow Dave Clare had had a bit of a row with the Horse and Dave finished up with us.

By now Chang was anxious to get working alongside us in the lucrative protection racket, so we made arrangements with the various establishments we took care of. For the next few days we took Chang in tow when visiting our benefactors, most of whom realised what a lot our services had to offer any business, especially the illegal dives that had sprung up all over the place. Like everybody else who was involved with us in the protection racket, Chang realised that in the event of the Serious Crime Squad busting us we would be facing long terms of imprisonment.

Fortunately we never had many problems as most of our patrons could ill afford to have much attention drawn to themselves. Many were not adverse to buying and selling stolen spirits and cigarettes, and this was what drew some of them to our attention. I am not condoning our actions or trying to justify them, nor would I advise anybody to even think of trying this in the modern day and age. On reflection I think we had more than our share of good luck and also we were a bit selective and had a lot of help from our friends in the wings who posed a threat to anyone who lodged a complaint against us. Over the years some of us were often pulled in for questioning, and several times many of us landed up convicted of various offences such as malicious damage, GBH and demanding money with menaces. But these are the hazards of the extortion racket.

CHAPTER TEN

Rachman and Others

Throughout the mid-Fifties we would spent a lot of time in the West End, with Tommy Smithson in his spieler or in the billiard hall in Great Windmill Street, Piccadilly. On the floor above the billiard hall was Jack Solomon's office – at that time he had a virtual monopoly on the fight game. Very often we would bump into a Pole who was known as Serge Parplinski and several of his cronies who would often be found hanging around the gymnasiums watching boxers work out.

Later on we found out that Serge Parplinski was closely connected to Peter Rachman, the notorious landlord whose intimidation and exorbitant rent charges and various activities were well known to us. Rachman was a well-built man with a fat belly and he and his partner, a Lebanese named Raymond Nash, earned a fortune by letting out near-derelict premises for high rents in Bayswater and Paddington. To remove tenants from these slums he had an army of strong-arm men. Through him, the term Rachmanism became a household word. He lived off the misfortunes of other people and did not care whom he hurt in getting money into his pocket.

Our dealings with Rachman started around 1957 or 1958. Many

different gangs and individuals were involved with him in one capacity or another and some of us were aware of it and some not. We knew practically all that went on in the Notting Hill and Paddington areas so Rachman became of great interest to us, the more so as we heard that he was due to open and become the owner of the El Condor Club in Wardour Street. We spoke about the huge potential it had to Tommy Smithson, but he was not very interested as he was always a loner, although he was not averse to getting involved in a bit of freelance protection. Sadly poor Tommy died as he was blasted to death in 1958 by a shotgun-wielding gang of Maltese with whom he had fallen out. But true to his code, after being shot in the stomach at close range he tried to drag himself towards his killers in a futile bid for revenge. I always found Smithson an uncomplicated person who never put much value on the material things in life and who was very much a loner. He was strictly a heterosexual man who disliked being with homosexuals in case people drew the wrong conclusions.

In the beginning of 1960 Big Dave Clare, who was a member of our firm and came out of Walthamstow where his mother ran a wet fish stall in the market, was driving me in my Jag along Hackney Road when I saw Ronnie Kray and a couple of young fellas walking along 50 yards or so in front of us. I asked Big Dave to slow down and told him that for the past couple of months or so many people had been approaching me in the West End and East London saying the Krays wanted to see me. I was sure they were not satisfied with the beating I had taken over the Terry Martin affair and wanted to extract some more vengeance.

I went on to say, 'As you know, Dave, I've had a lot of aggravation with the Krays over the past few years, or more particularly from that one [meaning Ronnie Kray] who's a fucking raving space cadet whose mind's so fucked up you can't talk sense to the man.' I continued, 'I'm getting a bit pissed off with forever being told the Krays want to see me so I want to settle this once and for all and have a confrontation. I realise we're outnumbered, but the other two young guys are probably just a couple of young fellas he's humping so they won't cause any problem.' I asked Dave, 'Well, how do you feel? Shall we stop and give him a pull or what?' Dave replied, 'Yeah. Why not?' So he drove the Jag alongside the trio and I wound the window down, saying, 'How are you doing?'

Ronnie looked over and approached the car. I made sure the window was only partially open. He looked at Dave then into the back of the car and when he saw we were alone he said, 'What way are you going? Can you drive us to the billiard hall?' I said, 'Yeah, we're going that way.' So the three of them piled into the back. No one spoke for several minutes then Ronnie Kray pulled out a pack of cigarettes and said to Dave, 'Do you want a cigarette?' Dave said, 'No.' Then Ronnie said to me, 'Do *you* want one?' I noticed the double meaning and the venom in his voice and realised I had made a mistake, so I nudged Dave's leg with my knee to let him know we were probably going to have a battle on our hands. By now we had turned into Eric Street, Mile End, and on to the bit of waste ground in front of the billiard hall. As we pulled on to it I noticed Reggie Kray was on the steps leading to the billiard hall and several others of the firm were in close vicinity, and beginning to move towards us with obvious intent.

As soon as the car came to a halt I threw open the passenger door as did Dave the driver's door. I began to lash out with a small, lethal springloaded lead cosh then made good my escape. They all came for me together so I ran into Burdett Road with them after me and jumped on the platform of a passing bus, still lashing out at my pursuers with the weapon. Fortunately the bus driver didn't stop to see what all the commotion was. After a few minutes I got off the bus, took a cab to Stamford Hill and made a round of all the clubs and other establishments that Dave would be likely to head for – but without success. By now I was beginning to be concerned for Dave's safety. By 11 p.m. I still had not located him so I phoned the Krays' club, the Double R, and asked to speak to Reg Kray. When he came to the phone I said, 'It's Billy Webb here. What's become of my pal?' To which he replied, 'I don't know.' Then he said, 'Let's forget it. Come over and have drink.' I said, 'How can I? I've got no fucking motor.' He must have thought I said no money because he said, 'You're joking, we'll forget the money side of it.'

I thought I could trust Reggie to a degree and I was so worried about Dave I threw caution to the wind. I managed to start up a car I hadn't used for weeks and made my way over to the Double R. I had done a couple of deals with Reggie whilst Ronnie was away on the Bobby Ramsey charge, helping him out with a couple of people who had been giving him some aggravation. I thought I was on pretty safe ground and it was either take Reggie at his word or be forever looking over my shoulder. There was no question of involving other people – if I went to the Double R with strength in numbers it would undoubtedly have ended in all-out war. As I drove over there all manner of things were going through my mind.

Big Pat Connelly was on the door and as I stepped inside the club I looked around me. Most of the customers I was on first name terms with. Quite a few nodded their heads in acknowledgment. Some of the others were only assholes so I never paid them any heed. Over the years I'd had plenty of battles with some of them and maimed a few so they would have liked to get a bit of the action against me if the balloon went up. A minute or so later Reggie was at my side asking what I'd like to drink and I had a dry martini and tonic. Now I was in the midst of the Kray camp. I realised I would have to be a bit selective about voicing my opinions but at the same time retain my dignity. Many of the Kray firm must have been surprised to see me walk into the club on my own. Suddenly I glimpsed mad Ronnie with a couple of young boys whom he was most probably humping. By now he must have wondered where Reggie had got to as he was looking around the bar. Although I was facing Reggie whilst we were talking I could see exactly what was going on at the far end of the bar where Ronnie was sitting. Within a minute or so he had joined us saying as he approached, 'How are you?' His manner had changed. Nothing was mentioned about the advance payment I had had off them for the unfulfilled contract on Terry Martin.

Ronnie asked who was the guy who was with me earlier that day. Reggie said, 'From up north?' I replied, 'No he's pretty local', still wondering what the fuck had happened to him. By now

Ronnie must have been anxious to get back to his two young friends and left our company. I was pretty surprised and puzzled at his change of attitude. I said to Reggie, 'Ronnie was well out of order digging my pal out', to which he replied, 'Well, he was in your company', which he seemed to think was reason enough. I learned they did not know of Dave's whereabouts so I left the Double R thinking at least he was probably still alive, and began my search of all the spielers, clubs and pubs that I often frequented with Big Dave, again without success.

The following evening I was parking outside the all-night restaurant at Stamford Hill when all of a sudden Dave was standing alongside the car smiling all over his face saying, 'We fucked their little plot up, didn't we?' I was all the more pleased to see his face was unmarked and I said, 'Where the fuck you been, Dave?' He replied, of all things, 'I just went over to Walthamstow to see my mother!'

When I told him how I had gone back to the Double R looking for him he couldn't believe I had done that on my own. He said, 'What the fuck – you put your life on the line.' Looking back I can see that I may have done, although I was not entirely alone – I was carrying a piece and wouldn't have gone down quietly. And at least I had got the Krays off my back for the meantime as they had been reminded I was not someone who was easily intimidated.

At about this time we heard that Peter Rachman had several gambling clubs, all illegal, with no drinks licences or gaming licences, and that made him of great interest to us. We had known for some time that Rachman was not at all organised, as all his muscle were only drifters and dossers who were merely part-time amateurs offering no threat to anyone. Many of the people he used to carry out his intimidation and violence used to socialise together in various clubs I used myself like The Alphabet and The Fiesta in Notting Hill. Jack 'The Hat' McVitie would also frequent these clubs.

Rachman was without doubt a clever and ruthless man who used intimidation as a means of getting everything he wanted. Just like the Krays, he knew that if people are afraid enough, you can get whatever you want. But when any of that violence was directed against him he was very vulnerable. He also did not like publicity. To us he was fair game.

For several nights we would show ourselves in force at his 150 Club in Earls Court Road and the New Court Club where the gambling took place in the basement which boasted the one chemin de fer table. Of course when we started frequenting his spielers many of his regular patrons began to drift away. This did not go unnoticed by Rachman so it was inevitable that shortly he would be approaching us. Serge Parplinski was often with him, so Rachman had no doubt as to who we were and undoubtedly knew the reasons for our intrusion.

On a couple of occasions we would send a few of our firm over to Notting Hill to kidnap a few of his hookers and beat his rent collectors up for good measure, which did not go down well with Rachman. We were also visiting his other club, the El Condor in Wardour Street, which was often frequented by the so called upper bracket. This was being run by Raymond Nash and he was not too pleased when we made an appearance there. The outcome of our efforts was that we got a percentage of the takings at both the 150 Club and the New Court Hotel. We put in two of our own croupiers who would complete a shoe in five or six minutes faster than their predecessors – so the takings were up and so, in a sense, we unwittingly gave a good service to Rachman. This arrangement went on for a couple of years.

I don't know of anyone who got much change out of Rachman. We never got enough to alter our lifestyle very much. Sometimes he would just disappear so we had to devise our own ways to get our dues. He was good at disappearing to get out of trouble or get out of paying and got the name of Runaway Rachman. Finally we became a bit disillusioned with Rachman and his Pimpernel acts. I knew that Rachman was also dealing with the Krays and it would be only a matter of time before they would be sniffing around. So we decided to put some distance between ourselves and Rachman.

Around 1958 we started frequenting The Cosmopolitan drinking club in Stoke Newington, Hackney, and bleeding the owner dry. The club was unlicensed and to a passer-by would be mistaken as a shop or small manufacturing premises. It was being run by a tall young guy called Peter Jones. The opposition was non-existent at that time so we arranged for several of our fringe members to cause havoc. Every night we arranged for fights to break out and subsequently there were a lot of breakages. So when we suggested to Peter Jones that we would guarantee that we would put an end to all the fighting for a consideration, he readily agreed. After that nobody who was in our company paid for their drinks and just about anyone in our firm could go and nip the owner for a tenner.

A couple of hundred yards along the road was The Regency Club which the Krays often used. Soon after we had started looking after the Cosmopolitan Club Ronnie Kray had finished his three-year sentence and was back on the streets. But at this time when the Krays were using The Regency Club I always made sure I had a couple of tried and trusted pals nearby. Billy Welsh was mostly at hand and he really despised the Kray twins. I also made sure I had someone in the near vicinity carrying a lethal weapon for me should the opportunity arise to settle the score. But I knew this was nigh impossible as the twins were always mob-handed and never dared venture anywhere on their own because over the years they had taken many liberties of a diabolical nature and were really loathed and hated by many people, many of whom were straight businessmen whose lives were in ruins. There were also many thieves who had trusted the Krays to fence their stolen goods and finished up with a paper hat.

Unbeknown to us, the owner of The Cosmopolitan approached the Krays with the notion that he could set up a deal with them to oust us. He never realised that by doing this he was virtually handing over the keys of the club to the Krays, and that overnight he would be demoted to the boy that served the drinks, paid the bills and whatever other demands the Krays made.

I should imagine that Ronnie Kray was in his glory to hear of the existence of The Cosmopolitan, which was a new club that had gone unnoticed by them. He would be ecstatic (depending on his mood) to know that I was connected with the club and thought that he could score off me again. When he was told that we were into the club owner, I should imagine the owner gave the Krays all the information as to when we would be in the club, how many of us there would be and if we were armed. So one night the twins came to The Cosmopolitan to sort us out.

However, due to something that cropped up unexpectedly, Ron and I were not at The Cosmopolitan when they struck. Poor Chang and a few of our pals were there and took the brunt of it. As usual they came in numbers so our lot had no chance. They all took a terrible beating, most of all Chang, whom they picked out because they knew he was a close friend of ours. After beating him they tied him to a chair and threw the chair and him down two flights of stairs. Fortunately, he was not tipped over headlong, but sideways. Nevertheless, the broken bones and fractures he had were numerous and when I next saw Chang he was in a terrible state.

Shortly after this incident Ron, Chang and me were taken in and questioned by the murder squad as to our whereabouts a day or two prior to being picked up. At this time I was living in a ground-floor furnished flat facing Clapton Common in Stamford Hill. It was about midday and I had only been up about ten minutes as I had been out all night. I remember looking for a fresh towel in a cupboard by the door leading to the communal hallway when several men burst in with guns pointing. One man shouted, 'Don't move! Stay where you are!' I found myself with two guns pointed only inches from my head and heard someone shout, 'Cuff him!' My hands were cuffed behind my back and I was jostled out into the hallway.

The place was swarming with uniformed police. Two were at the top of the stairs, a couple in the hallway, plus the three plainclothes who had captured me. I was held in the hallway whilst they searched my flat, though they only gave it a quick spin. Then a police car arrived outside and I was bundled into it. Within five minues or so I was in Stoke Newington Police Station. I was put in a cell, then finally taken out and interviewed about a murder. I had a bit of a problem about the time they were interested in. I was evasive and said I had been in the West End drinking heavily. I realised only too well that they could not hold

Having my collar felt, 1993

Our mum posing as Marlene Dietrich in a borrowed army uniform

*My Cadillac Coup de Ville – the terror of London pimps, especially
Maltese Joe, one of the many forced to leave the city*

My brother Ron with his wife, Anne

Painting by brother Ron

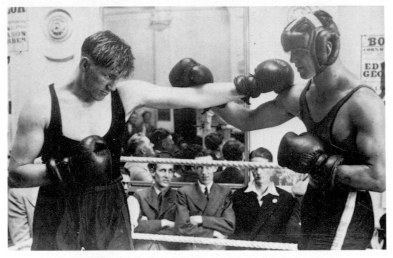

Tommy 'The Bear' Brown (right), *sparring with Tommy Farr*

*'The Bear' went on to become the number one minder in the Kray firm –
sentenced to three years for GBH when the Krays received their
30-year sentence*

From left to right: *Johnny Squib (Judy Garland's husband), Judy Garland, Reg Kray, Ronnie Kray and guests, 1963*

Reggie Kray and Billy Hill in Tangiers

The George and Dragon – where George Cornell gave Ronnie Kray a terrible beating

The basement flat where Jack the Hat was lured to by the Lambrianous and stabbed to death

1ST. JULY

H.M. PRISON,
PARKHURST,
NR. NEWPORT,
ISLE OF WIGHT

Dear Bill
THANKS for your letter.
Bill I CAN'T REMEMBer

we used to Have.
only THE one
PROSPECT.
Lets HOPe in the
Future, we will
Have Some nice times
TOGETHer.
Bill will you try
to get me Some NICE
PHOTOS of Boys.
For my ALBUM.
I will Be most
reatfull if you can
P.T.O

No. 243 30141 8-2-68

Letter to me from Ronnie Kray

From left to right: *Reg Kray, John Wakefield, Ron Webb, Dickie Morgan*

With my daughter, Deborah

With Bobby Ramsey

me indefinitely but I was worried that the more they held on to me the more they would start probing into what we were doing.

They kept saying, 'We know what you're at but we are not concerned with that. All we want is to clear up this murder, and the sooner we eliminate you the sooner you'll be out in the sunshine and fresh air.' They kept on emphasising this, but I didn't believe them for an instant. If they had found out anything about me they would have passed it on to their fellow officers. I knew only too well that no stone is left unturned in a murder case, so the sooner we got out the better. By this time I found out that Ron and Chang had also been captured and were in the cells.

This caused us a problem as we were all held in separate cells and our arrests had come unexpectedly. Like me, Ron and Chang must have been experiencing the same dilemma – we realised once we told them the truth as to our whereabouts that there was every chance we would be busted. There was no way I could find out or even hazard a guess as to what Ron and Chang would say. I got the impression the law knew more about our ways of life than they were letting on and that they were just playing it down. I knew that whatever alibi we came up with would be checked and seeing as we knew nothing about any murder we had no prepared alibi. Our big problem was that the longer they held us the deeper they would probe into our illegal activities.

I knew from past experience that as one team of detectives was questioning me other teams of police would be interrogating Ron and Chang and at the end of each session they would compare notes. It was all very puzzling and I was racking my brains as to whom we had hurt recently that was bad enough to result in a death, but for some time now things had been running smoothly.

I knew one of us would have to take the initiative – the sooner they started checking the alibi the sooner they would stop making enquiries of their own. So I began by making a statement. I told them that at the time in question we were around the Bayswater Road and Edgware Road looking for a hooker who had turned Chang over. I never told them the real reason we were there, which was that we were rolling Maltese Joe's hustlers or, as the hookers liked to say, they were being 'kidnapped'. At the time of all this my yellow Cadillac was easily recognised and known everywhere, especially by the hookers. Undoubtedly the police would confirm it was in the vicinity at the time.

As the murder they were investigating had happened in Walthamstow, I started thinking about Dave Clare. He came from that area. I thought maybe something was going on that I didn't know about as Dave was the newest addition to the firm. It was a bit of a predicament. It was all very well the interrogators saying all they wanted to do was clear up this murder and eliminate us and that they were not concerned with anything except murder, but I couldn't buy the idea that they were trying to sell me. So I stuck to my story. Finally they put me back in the cell where I stayed for a few hours lying on the bed trying to make some sense of the situation. It did enter my mind that someone I had had dealings with in the past was trying to fit us up and it wouldn't be beyond the Krays to have done such a thing to finish off the episode of The Cosmopolitan.

I finally began to feel a bit sleepy and started dozing off when suddenly I heard someone opening the cell door. Next thing I knew I was ushered into a small room where Ron and Chang were seated. The Old Bill seemed to have the right hump with me. I fully expected to have the customary caution read out to me and to be charged, instead of which I learned that whilst we were in the cells they had been making enquiries and were satisfied we were not involved. A couple of weeks later I read the details in the newspaper. The Mayor of Hackney had been kidnapped and forced to open the safe of his office and hand over £8,000. The shock was too much and he died of heart failure. The verdict was 'manslaughter by a person or persons unknown'.

Because Ronnie had just finished doing his three years I was convinced he had fitted us up and as far as I know no one has ever been nicked for the incident.

Once again Maltese Joe was causing us a few problems and we decided to hit him where it hurts most, 'in the pocket', by getting some of our firm to roll his hookers. It was easy enough with a driver and someone in the back seat and the hookers got in readily and handed over their takings. I heard that many of them found it a bit exciting to be what they now termed being 'kidnapped'. Of course we made sure that none of the girls were harmed. I think I can honestly say that being 'kidnapped' was exciting for them and gave them an excuse to hold back a bit of money from Maltese Joe. After a couple of months they became a bit disenchanted with Maltese Joe who had practically no backing apart from his younger brother and two cousins, so he slowly began to lose his grip as he had lost favour in their eyes by allowing the situation to continue and not hitting back.

There was the occasional mistake such as when a schoolteacher thought she was being offered a lift, got into the back seat of the car and was a bit outraged to be asked for her money. And one of our firm went out and rolled one of the hookers on his own and got cut by the Maltese mob who thought he was going freelance. But eventually we finished up driving the small-time pimp out of London. Nobody knows for sure what became of him but whatever the outcome we certainly brought a lot of excitement to certain hookers and several parts of London and maybe we unintentionally helped one or two girls out of the clutches of Maltese Joe and out of the miserable lives they were living. We may have even inadvertently helped the vice squad in a small way by cleaning up some streets of London and ridding the capital of Maltese Joe and his little firm of small-time pimps who had eluded them for so long.

During these years we were often approached by straight businessmen who were anxious for us to do their dirty work for them, ranging from arson, frame-ups, arranging for a burglar or specialist safebreaker to ransacking a business rival's premises, to murder. I have known supposedly shrewd businessmen sit down and join me and Ron at a table in a high-class restaurant and outline plans and details of exactly what they wanted doing. After the meeting they would walk off leaving us with all their plans in their own handwriting, never thinking for a moment that from then on we would have a grip on them.

Believe me, when it gets around that your firm will carry out a personal service you get all sorts of requests and you have to take the play away from the individuals and assure them that they are talking to the right people who will solve their problems for a price. Once when I was in The Regency Club I had a woman whisper in a low voice that she wanted someone to kill her wealthy husband who, it seemed, had a weakness for the ladies. She in turn had a toy-boy. I knew she was deadly serious as she had every item worked out to the smallest detail. One screwball even wanted to be murdered himself so his family could claim the insurance money.

High on the hit list of many businessmen was Ronnie Kray. Many criminals and businessmen wanted him out of the way. In particular there was one man whom the Krays had been blackmailing for a year or more and who eventually had to sell up and move to another part of the country to start his life anew. But Ronnie was always too heavily surrounded by minders. He was later to write in a newspaper article that I never had the courage to sort him out, but the truth was that no one could get anywhere near him. Many, including me, did try.

One Jewish businessman we worked for, a Mr Polkov, owned vast residential properties in Stoke Newington and ran his rented accommodation along the same lines as Peter Rachman. Like Rachman, he had a weakness for blondes if he could get his way by bullying them. In those days there was no race relations board and a landlord could advertise 'No children, pets or coloureds'. But Polkov wanted to feel that he had some backing to rely on if a situation arose so he made some arrangements with us. We knew we had backing from certain of the Old Bill who were not averse to a little bit of extra cash.

Polkov would arrange for us to visit premises where he was having problems to throw out the tenants and change the locks. If we knocked on the door of a person who was in arrears in rent we would sometimes be confronted by three or four blacks sharing the one room that was being let as a single, in which case we either turfed them out or the rent was increased fourfold, which suited Polkov. In the case of locks being changed this was no cost to Polkov as he had an abundance of locks from other premises, so he merely chopped and changed them.

We acquired our club in Shacklewell Lane by courtesy of Mr

Polkov. It suited him to know he could get hold of members of our firm at short notice. The premises he gave us access to we turned into a spieler and drinking club. It had been a shop at one time, amidst other commercial premises, which suited us fine. Polkov had his own maintenance staff so we insisted on them repairing broken windows and other minor jobs and we coaxed them into doing the painting and decorating. We installed Big Scotch Willie Gregory on the door to charge an admission fee to strangers. Scotch Willie occupied one of the upstairs rooms that we had furnished so he was always in attendance. Occasionally Chang or Billy Welsh would stand in. Of course we had teething problems and our share of layabouts who treated the club as their second home, but these people would fetch and carry for us. Soon one of them had helped build a bar and we had half a dozen or more card tables. Walls were knocked down and within a few weeks it was a going concern. A full-size snooker table was installed for shooting craps (American dice) and a factory clock was timing the table money. The most popular games were rummy, poker, and kalooki (a form of rummy with 13 cards).

We were open 24 hours a day and 80 to a hundred people would come in during that time. Our big nights were Friday and Saturday. Georgie Lane served tea and coffee and snacks on the ground floor and on the first floor we had a drinking club. The organisation was pretty big and many of our close friends and allies came from places like Hornsey, Walthamstow and Wood Green. In those days we lived a hard code. This club helped to feed the many mouths we needed to keep our firm alive. The protection rackets were widespread, there was plenty of work – and any we did for Polkov was paid well and in advance.

CHAPTER ELEVEN

Why They Shot George Cornell

During the Sixties, Ron and I were making deals and socialising with many people from South London. Everyone we dealt with knew of Ronnie Kray's madness and everyone tried to give the twins a wide berth. This was when the Krays were extending their operations into South London. Reggie Kray had once told me that he had served time in an army prison with one of the Richardson brothers and the Krays were a bit peeved that the Richardsons were into various things in South London. The Richardsons had a good legitimate business in scrap metal yards and they also had a legitimate wholesale chemist's business. But they were greedy and branched out into protection of clubs and businesses and ran some crooked companies dealing in goods of all sorts. The Krays felt they should be allowed into these enterprises. But the Richardsons were much too wise – in comparison to their set-up, the Krays were a couple of pan-handlers. An enmity began.

One night a raiding party shot up a pub in Bethnal Green five minutes after the twins had left. Another time a car waiting in Vallance Road drove on to the pavement and knocked down a man who looked like Ronnie. The Krays put all this down to the Richardsons and they started wearing bullet-proof waistcoats.

Then they bought two Browning machine-guns for £75 each. They took them down to the south coast to practise firing shots into the sea.

Whereas the Richardsons had a big following of loyal, trusted, ruthless men, such as George Cornell and Frank Fraser, the Krays lacked anyone of that calibre except for The Bear. But as game and strong as The Bear was, he would only use his fists and brute strength on a man and would never use a tool. The twins had tried their hardest to induce The Bear's brother, Billy, to join their firm but he hated the pair of them and tried to get his brother to sever all relations with them. The rest of the Kray firm was always changing and couldn't be relied on. If they left the firm they were beaten and cut. Some just disappeared off the face of the earth and are still on Scotland Yard's missing persons list. When he was asked how many other killings the Krays had committed, Inspector Nipper Read, who led the Scotland Yard team which finally nicked the Krays, said on television that the team had investigated seven murders. I was on this same programme with Nipper Read and can confirm this.

In the early Sixties one of our firm was Chris Lambrianou, who lived with his parents and his younger brother, Tony, in a ground-floor flat in a block of council flats in Queensbridge Road, off Hackney Road. We met him through Scouse Eddie who was friendly with Tony Lambrianou. They became the famous Lambrianou brothers who got 15 years' imprisonment for helping Reggie Kray to murder Jack 'The Hat' McVitie after luring him from The Regency Club to the flat where he was murdered.

When Chris Lambrianou joined our firm he was a drifter trying to get into something. So he moved around with us for a short time but we never got deeply involved as we knew too little about him. He was useful sometimes and would oblige us by agreeing to let us keep the odd weapon at his flat where it was pretty safe and saved us the risk of having any lethal weapons found in our car. But I never really trusted him.

At this time I was on good terms with a fella called Charlie Olsen who would occasionally accompany me and Chang or whoever was available to collect the dues owed for looking after one establishment or another. On one particular occasion I could not find Chang's whereabouts and for some reason or another no one was available except Chris Lambrianou. So Chris, Charlie Olsen and I went to a cafe in Commercial Road, Stepney. I didn't give the matter much thought as there were seldom any problems with this cafe, but I was not aware that Chris's knowledge in this field was limited. After arriving at the restaurant Chris and Charlie Olsen had gone in front of me whilst I was parking the car and suddenly all hell had broken loose in the cafe. I ran in to see what had happened and found all the tables and chairs overturned and the place a wreck. The pintable was smashed and the floor was knee-deep in broken glass, cups and plates.

Next thing I knew we were all nicked for malicious damage. It appeared that Lambrianou had got things confused and fucked everything up, as the governor of the cafe was on holiday and Lambrianou thought he was refusing to pay. When Ron heard, he went berserk. But there was nothing he could do in straightening things out as it was now a police matter. When the proprietor came back we managed to put the frighteners on him with the aid of the appearance at the restaurant of a few heavies as a deterrent. But although the proprietor said he did not want to press charges the police had other ideas. I got arrested with Chris and Charlie and it cost me £300 to bribe the police not to oppose my bail.

We eventually appeared at Arbour Square Magistrates Court and the magistrate sentenced us all to six months for malicious damage. He would have liked to have given us six years if it was in his power as throughout the trial the police dropped subtle hints as to protection rackets going on at that time. They were well aware that Ron had fixed things and were a bit peeved about it all.

We lost no time in getting rid of Chris Lambrianou and had a laugh when we learnt he was a stooge for the Krays, thanks to the recommendation of our friend, Johnny Gardner, who was known as Johnny 'The Eyes' for his deep-set penetrating eyes.

I was sent to Pentonville prison, otherwise known as the Ville. On arrival I and my fellow cons were bolted up in small cubicles where we had to discard our clothes and throw them outside. Then a brief inspection was made by the prison doctor. We had to bathe in about six inches of lukewarm water, were given our prison garb and were bolted up for the night. Next morning the Prison Governor allocated our prison jobs. You have no say in the matter and cannot pick or choose. I was not surprised to find myself sewing mail-bags at eight stitches to the inch. I've sat alongside men who have spent five or six years and even eight years doing nothing day in and day out except sewing mail-bags at eight stitches to the inch, no more or less. It's all so degrading and soul-destroying, but come rain or shine they sit there working with the needle trying to achieve their quota in order to receive the weekly pittance of pay.

I was one of the fortunate ones who did not depend on the weekly pay pittance, but being a compassionate person in many instances I like to think I made life a bit easier for my friends whilst they were serving their prison sentences alongside me by helping them with a bit of tobacco. In prison tobacco is the equivalent to money, and from day one of my sentence I always had plenty of tobacco which was acquired through bent screws and from outside working parties. What counts on the outside is how much money you have and what connections you have, in prison it's who you are and how much tobacco you've got. Subsequently, I had a cell of my own and was not sharing with two others, and I had my own personal valet in the form of a landing cleaner who fetched and carried for me and kept my cell neat and tidy.

In those days prison rules and regulations were much different than they are today. Every prisoner was allowed one visit per month and allowed to write and receive one letter per fortnight. Sometimes the prison censors would turn a blind eye to any extra letters you received, within reason. Other times the letter would be returned to the sender.

Sending out letters caused no problems and Ron would occasionally arrange a one-off visit, courtesy of the prison welfare department. Nowadays things are entirely different. Lifers and category 'A' prisoners are now walking about the prison in Lonsdale sweatshirts and jeans. These are maximum security prisons I'm talking about.

There's now no such thing as security in a maximum security

prison. I've received phone calls from so-called maximum security prisoners and once from a prisoner in transit from one maximum security prison to another. But if a man is serving several years for fraud, theft or any minor felony he is subjected to all the prison rules and regulations. At the other end of the scale, if a man kills in cold blood he has many privileges that are denied to the lesser felon. Strange as it seems, it is a fact. This all seems a bit ludicrous to me, but the penal system's workings always did baffle me. I could never fathom out why they opt to degrade a man by giving him a needle and thread to sew mail-bags by hand year after year when the same task could be done by machine.

But as I said earlier on, I was not dependent on any prison earnings so would often pay fellow cons to do my day's quota. And some of the time I managed to persuade the doctor I was ill. I was prescribed the normal aspirin and had a few days in my cell unfit for work. Ron managed to get a few extra visits from the welfare officer and kept me up to date with all that was going on outside. I wasn't surprised to learn that some of the access letters that had been sent to me had been sent back, as recently I'd slagged off and belittled a screw known as Speedy in front of a couple of other screws. So I finished up in the chokey block and lost three days' remission. Most probably he had something to do with my access mail being returned to sender – one of his pals worked in the censor's office.

I was really seething that someone could stoop so low. Getting back at someone by stopping their mail is despicable, but then Speedy Gonzales, as he was known, was despised throughout the prison even by most of the other screws. He got this nickname, which I think he revelled in, because he took great pride in the number of cell doors he could bolt up in a given time. I realise it all seems a bit stupid but he wasn't all that bright.

Fortunately all screws are not like Speedy Gonzales – some you can have a deal with. There was one whom I had met outside some time ago in a drinking club that was being run by a pal of mine called Buller Ward (who some years later was also cut up pretty bad by the Krays). This particular screw, who for obvious reasons should remain nameless, would bring me practically anything I, or anyone he could trust, wanted. He would also take out stiffs (smuggled outgoing letters). Mind you, some of these services didn't come cheap as he was running a bit of a risk.

The end of my sentence came without me making too many waves. I already knew a lot of the cons there when I arrived and I made the acquaintance of a few more whom I told to look us up at the completion of their sentences. After my release a few, whom I trusted enough to give an address, would often drop me a line and we would occasionally visit them. Others would return to their home town of Manchester, Glasgow or wherever.

Although being released from prison is a wonderful experience that words cannot explain, I still felt a bit sad at some of those I left behind. When I stepped out of the gates Ron was there waiting for me with a couple of pals. I couldn't get into the car quick enough. They were all a bit tired as they had been up in a spieler all night so that they would not oversleep and leave me in there a minute more than necessary.

As usual we drove to my mother's house. I could see they were all dead beat so I never forced a conversation about all that had been happening since I had been away. The rest of the day I spent at home with our mum and stepfather as this is what I wanted. Ron's pals were Wally Gore, whom Ron had nicknamed 'The Map' as he knew almost every street and square in London, especially the spielers and clubs in the West End, and Johnny Gardner, whom Ron had nicknamed 'The Eyes'. These nicknames were to stick to them like the various names he thought of for other people we became involved with. It was just a natural thing for someone to say, 'Have you seen The Map?' or 'I haven't seen The Eyes lately'. Many people never even knew these guys' surnames and it just came natural. I've not no idea how Chang got his nickname and to most people he was only known as Chang.

In the mid-Sixties the protection racket was at a peak. If any of our mob saw an easy mark like a restaurant, we would arrange to cause havoc. After a lot of subtle hints had been spread around the owner would approach us and offer a sum of money to ensure that the establishment would remain peaceful. Our organisation had grown in numbers of tried and trusted men and the police were trying to infiltrate it in various guises. But their hands were tied as no one establishment would come forward unless we were all in police custody at one time, which was virtually impossible as many of our confederates were unknown by name to our benefactors. By now the Krays were putting themselves out to be friendly and we were seeing a lot of them.

At the time I found Reggie not too bad as I'd heard that the order to have me cut up had come from his twin brother Ronnie. At this time Ronnie was getting worse and both of them were very argumentative towards each other. If Reggie was on the gin he would often burst into tears. When they were under the influence of drugs like purple hearts, their moods differed. Reggie would be happy and jovial but when the drugs wore off he would be depressed. Reggie took many more pills than his twin. Pills never seemed to have much effect on Ronnie who was always slagging someone off with or without booze or drugs. I've never seen either of them in a drunken stupor. They were both too frightened to drop their guard as they knew that over the years they had made so many enemies. There would never be a shortage of people who would be keen to get their own back if they found the twins drunk and unable to call up their protectors.

One of the places we were looking after at this time was a cafe in Church Street, Stoke Newington. In January 1966 the owner of the cafe was beginning to get a bit brave and he told a friend he wasn't going to pay his dues (protection money). Chang and another one of our firm called John Whewell decided he needed a bit of a roughing up. So in the early hours they went to the cafe and smashed it up. I don't know if it's true or not, but the police alleged that when they came into the cafe, Chang went up to a group of boys playing on a football machine and smashed one of them in the face. Whewell then took all the money from the till, threw vodka over the owner's wife and pulled out a knife and threatened to cut up her pet dogs. They then threatened to set fire to the place. Soon after Chang and Whewell got away the police pounced and the gang-busters were called in. All the customers in the cafe were questioned but no one was prepared to come forward and make statements.

Chang and John Whewell were arrested and remanded in custody. We learnt that no more charges were being brought against them so we realised our wall of silence had not been broken. But the police were still putting the pressure on. Seeing as I was the only other one directly involved in the incident I had to keep a low profile, but we could not lose a grip of the situation because of a slight hiccup, so as stressful as it was, I had to be seen at large in the various establishments with Ron or Billy Welsh. This counteracted any move by the police to assure our benefactors that everything was under control and the organisation smashed.

Chang and Whewell were eventually sent for trial at the Old Bailey charged with malicious damage, robbery and demanding money with menaces. They were refused bail on the grounds that they would threaten witnesses, although the police couldn't produce any witnesses except for Tom Bolton, the proprietor, and his wife. Two girls who were in the cafe told the police that they would sooner die than give evidence.

In April 1966 Chang and John Whewell appeared at the Old Bailey. At the trial the police said that because of what had happened the cafe owner's wife had attempted to commit suicide. They were both found guilty and sentenced to five years apiece. Shortly after they were convicted a warrant was put out for my arrest in the same case for demanding money with menaces.

As soon as I heard this, I went into hiding. I stayed in my Uncle Arthur's flat in Hoxton for a couple of months. I had my own key so I could come and go as I pleased. I had a Jaguar car then which was not known to the police. I spent all this time moving around with my cousins, Chrissie Hawkins and Punchy Hines in Whitechapel and Aldgate, which were pretty safe districts for me.

At this time I was friendly with George Cornell (whose real name was George Myers) who was working with Charlie and Eddie Richardson in South London. Cornell was a fighting man with many convictions for violence. Once he got three years for cutting a girl petrol station attendant. He was a bit of a loner and mostly he would be on his own but I got on with him and we often had a drink or two together. We had various sorts of business and financial deals with George Cornell. Things usually went smoothly between me and Cornell but sometimes, as can be expected, we had disagreements. But when he was in the wrong he would be the first to admit it. We spent a lot of time together in the Old Basing, a pub in Kingsland Road, Shoreditch, in the heart of Kray territory.

The Krays have said a lot about why Cornell was shot but have never admitted the real reasons. The truth is that in the early Sixties Cornell gave Ronnie Kray a terrible beating. It was so ferocious that some members of the Kray firm walked in fear of Cornell. Ronnie had never forgiven him. The reason Cornell gave him the beating was that Ronnie Kray had been doing business with Ginger Marks, who was a friend of mine. He was a fence and a dealer in stolen cars, which he sold on to George Cornell. He also did a lot of business with the Krays and it was while he was dealing with Ronnie Kray that Ginger suddenly disappeared. He was last seen in Cheshire Street near the stall of the Krays' uncle which was near a pub that the Krays often used. Shortly after Ginger was last spotted, some gunshots were heard in Cheshire Street and Ginger was never seen again. Almost everyone said the Krays were involved in this. Some say he was the Krays' first victim because he refused to be manipulated.

Two other friends of Ronnie Kray who vanished off the face of the earth were Teddy Smith, known as 'Mad Teddy', and a fella named Frost. It was Teddy who gave the Krays the idea of getting Frankie Mitchell out of Dartmoor. Like Ronnie, 'Mad Teddy' Smith was a homosexual and it was a well known fact that he and Ronnie had a fierce argument over a boy when he and Ronnie had spent a weekend together with some young men. Frost made a futile attempt at blackmailing Ronnie about it and after that he was never seen again. It wasn't till 1967 that homosexuality became legal. Ronnie would often take boys he was bedding out of the country for weekends, for he dreaded being caught in England and this made him vulnerable to blackmail. 'Mad Teddy' Smith and Frost are still on Scotland Yard's missing persons list.

Cornell was a good friend of Ginger's and he was furious. From the day Ginger disappeared Cornell would belittle Ronnie in public at every opportunity and taunt him to his face whenever he saw him. He would refer to Ronnie as 'Queenie' and make any offensive remark about him that came to his mind, so he had to go. Once he approached the father of one of Ronnie's boyfriends and warned him of the sexual nature of his son's friendship. Later came the attack on Ronnie Kray in an East End pub called The George and Dragon. Ronnie was by himself and with no one to back him up he didn't retaliate and lost a tooth.

The Krays had known Cornell since the 1950s and at first they'd all been good friends. But the time came when Cornell moved over to South London and got involved with the Richardsons. Cornell was doing a lot of the Richardsons' really dirty work. He was hired to pull teeth out and give electric shocks to the testicles of the Richardsons' victims. It was then that things went bad between Cornell and the Krays. From then on George Cornell never had any time for the Krays and never showed them any respect or saw them as any threat. This did not go down well with the Krays. Then came the time when George gave Ronnie the beating.

George Cornell loathed Ronnie Kray and often said he'd like to get him on his own and, in his own words, 'tear him apart with my bare hands'. But Ronnie Kray was always surrounded by his minders. Cornell had so much contempt for Ronnie that he was completely carefree in whatever he said about him. He was constantly making open remarks about Ronnie's homosexuality and calling him a poof. He didn't care if there were Kray spies in the pub or club. There often were, for Ronnie had plenty of young boys he had bedded and others anxious to get news about anything that they could scurry back to Ronnie with in order to find a bit of favour. Most thieves and villains knew this and would talk in whispers when they talked about the Krays, and especially if they were slagging Ronnie off, but Cornell didn't care. I remember I often warned him when we were in a pub or club not to sit with his back to the door. But he always laughed and said that Ronnie was a slag and too afraid to tangle with him.

Then came the time when one of Ronnie's spies told him that Cornell had called him a fat poof and had put it around that

Ronnie Kray had only taken a young man with him on a trip to Newcastle to get him into bed. This got back to Ronnie, who already had Cornell on his murder list, so he decided the time had come for Cornell to go. And when Cornell said in the hearing of one of Ronnie's spies that 'the king is dead' he signed his own death warrant. This was when the twins were on remand in Brixton prison for demanding money with menaces, and Cornell was implying that Ronnie would get convicted. Ronnie heard about this after he was acquitted and put George on his murder list. George in turn heard about that but he still laughed about Ronnie Kray. He never took any precautions or changed his lifestyle one bit.

On the afternoon of the day in March 1966 when Ronnie Kray shot Cornell dead in the Blind Beggar, my brother, my cousin Chrissie and George Cornell were having a drink in the Old Basing House when George left saying he was going to visit a friend in the Whitechapel hospital, which is a only stone's throw from the Blind Beggar pub. He arranged to meet us the following day in the Six Bells in Commercial Street. He never kept that meeting for he was shot dead that night.

I got news that he had been shot within an hour and I knew straight away who the assassin was. Thanks to his spies, Ronnie knew just where to find Cornell when he made up his mind to kill him. Scotch Jack Dickson drove him and Ian Barrie to the Blind Beggar pub. Ronnie went into the pub with Ian Barrie. They both had guns. Even when Ronnie pointed the gun at his head, Cornell didn't flinch as he didn't think Ronnie Kray would have the nerve. 'You haven't got the bottle to do it,' he said and they were his last words. Cornell and I always got on well. He was not the animal that people are led to believe.

A couple of weeks after he was murdered, I got arrested on the money with menaces charge. During the lower court proceedings Ron found out that a detective sergeant who was involved in the case was bent and he was giving this bent copper large sums of money on the condition that I would not be committed for trial to the Old Bailey and that the case against me was dismissed at the lower court. In all I made about three appearances at North

London Magistrates Court. On the first occasion Tom Bolton, the cafe owner who was the main prosecution witness, did not attend in spite of the police claiming that he had assured them he would, so the case was adjourned.

On my second court appearance Tom Bolton still did not turn up even though he had been served with a witness summons. So, once again I was remanded and a further date set. For me and my solicitor this was becoming a farce.

Finally the prosecution witness was arrested on a warrant with a surety of £100 to force him to attend. I was dumbfounded when he was ushered into court. I didn't help matters when I verbally abused him. God only knows what was going through the magistrate's mind. Admittedly I never helped matters, so it was inevitable that I was committed for trial at the Old Bailey.

After the hearing we got hold of the detective sergeant. Ron was furious as it was becoming more apparent that the detective sergeant wanted a conviction and me off the streets as well as money, but this was not on. So, unbeknown to me, Ron arranged to meet the bent copper later on that evening in a pub called the Cock Tavern. In the meantime Ron knew a phone number that could put him in direct contact to a department in Scotland Yard who investigated corruption in the police force. On phoning the Yard and getting connected to the extension he required, he was asked the police officer's name and where he was stationed, but Ron was too wise to let on and merely arranged a meeting.

When the Old Bill arrived to meet Ron he explained all that had gone on between him and the bent copper whom he had arranged to meet at the specified time at the Cock Tavern. One of the Old Bill then handed Ron a bundle of banknotes, all numbered. They moved on to the Cock Tavern and entered separately. The Old Bill seated themselves unobtrusively at strategic positions and Ron stood at the bar and awaited the arrival of the bent copper. After a short while he arrived and joined Ron at the bar. Ron ordered the drinks and tackled him as to why he had gone this far with the case against me. He made many feeble excuses to which Ron replied, 'I'm getting the impression you want Billy off the streets and a feather in your cap.' He said this was not so, to which Ron replied, 'Well you had better see to it that my brother walks out of this. I've got £50 in my pocket so you had better do something.' The copper assured Ron he would, and Ron replied, 'Well let's do the business.' The copper said, 'It's better we go to the gents.' On entering the gents Ron put the £50 in the copper's hand and he put it in his pocket. On leaving the gents the law pounced on him, frisked him and found the £50 bribe. When asked where the money came from he replied, 'That fucking man put it there' – meaning Ron.

They then took the bent copper to Wood Green Police Station and I assume they questioned him. This caused a lot of speculation as to whether some other police unit had been probing into our activities, as many of the CID who were known to us had seldom been seen lately. Also the Richardsons' crime empire in South London had been smashed a couple of months prior to my arrest. We were well aware that most of our car numbers had been circulated as we were constantly getting pulled up for no apparent reason, so while this surveillance continued much use was made of London taxis who would drop us at a walking distance to wherever we had business. At this time any important meetings took place on a caravan site at Waltham Cross known as the Willows. Unfortunately for the police many of the travellers were friends of ours and very loyal and anti-police so the Old Bill never ventured on to the Willows as that would be considered trespassing.

On a couple of occasions I was questioned by the Old Bill who had nicked the bent detective sergeant. The one in charge of the investigation introduced himself as Superintendent Western. I learned that the bent copper had been suspended and in the event of him being charged Ron and I would be called to give evidence. After a couple of months had elapsed it seemed as though the police had given up or were keeping a very low profile. Then I was told a date had been set for my trial at the Old Bailey.

No more charges were made against me. Ron, Billy Welsh and several others were outside running things so there was not much to worry about. The jury was sworn in but my counsel did not feel it worthwhile challenging any of them. Before the trial began he asked that the jury leave the court. After it had left, my counsel informed the judge that he would like the jury to be aware that the bent copper was at the moment suspended. Then the prosecution objected on some point or other, saying that this matter should be kept from the jury. The judge sided with the prosecutor and the trial began.

By now I was really annoyed, more so when Tom Bolton, the prosecution witness, was called into the witness box to testify. Pretty soon he had all the jury in his pocket, as well as the judge who benevolently enquired if he was feeling OK and then went on to ask him if he would like a glass of water. It never helped my case any when I said, 'Why don't you offer him a drop of Scotch with it, you'd like that wouldn't you, Tom?' I realised by now this outburst was just what the prosecution wanted and, knowing how sensitive I was, they goaded me into more outbursts. If I'd had any sense I would have sacked my counsel there and then and defended myself. Finally, I got in the witness box and that really sealed my fate. There's nothing a judge hates more than a prisoner being arrogant and defiant and I could see I'd annoyed him. In the judge's summing up he said to the jury, 'You have before you a man who has not been gainfully employed for a number of years and yet he is running a Jaguar car!' The jury was only out for 20 minutes – having a smoke, I suppose – but even while they were out I never thought they would convict me. They did, and I ended up getting 18 months imprisonment.

My counsel advised me to appeal against conviction. I remember vividly one of the reasons was, word for word: 'I was refused leave to adduce evidence to the court about a police officer's demands for money, and that the police officer had been suspended from duty'. Today the case would have been slung out of court but in those days your solicitor or barrister would advise you not to accuse a police officer of telling lies but merely to say he was mistaken. The general public would not buy the idea that a seemingly upright police officer would fabricate evidence and lie under oath. That's why in those days there were so many innocent people in prison.

Even today the police are seen to be almost beyond suspicion. I am not anti-police, providing the policing is up to a high standard, but I am opposed to police officers investigating other police officers. The police are only human and it stands to reason that the superior investigating officer will feel favourable towards another officer and more often than not give him the benefit of the doubt. These matters are always dealt with on an internal level, so justice is never seen to be done.

At least I could be thankful that no one else was involved at the time, except Chang and Whewell who had been sentenced to five years apiece back in April. Ron came down to the cells to tell me that the police surveillance seemed to have ceased and things were pretty well back to normal. The visit only lasted a few minutes so we said our goodbyes. After that I was escorted to the cell in the basement of the Old Bailey where I stayed until the prison van arrived to take me and other prisoners to various prisons. The remand prisoners went to Brixton Prison and a couple of first offenders went to Wormwood Scrubs Prison. I finished up at Wandsworth Prison, which is known as the Hate Factory.

CHAPTER TWELVE

Why They Killed McVitie

At Wandsworth I was told I would be working in the tailor's shop. This was at least a cut above the mail-bag shop which was so freezing cold in winter that just holding a steel sewing needle in between your fingers was in itself an ordeal. The tailor's shop was pretty warm and had no fixed work quota.

When I arrived in Wandsworth in 1966 Eddie Richardson and a few of the Richardson gang were there. Frankie Fraser and John McVicar, who is now a successful journalist, were both there. Another con was a guy called Osborne, who was an associate of the Krays. I think it was because of this he was doing bird. On the outside I had never got on with Osborne. Like me he was assigned to the tailor's shop to work and as soon as I laid eyes on him I knew I would have to beat the flashiness out of him. Anyway, I wasn't standing any flashiness from one of the Kray firm. Besides that he had been a party to hurting a friend of mine on the outside and positively knew that I would be seeking revenge. So he went out of his way to be nice by giving me sickening smiles and asked me if there was anything I needed – knowing deep in his heart that it was his blood I was after.

For several weeks I nursed my thoughts of revenge then finally I saw him walking along a landing. I lay in wait for him in a recess and as he passed I dragged him in by the scruff of the neck and smashed his head against the brick wall several times until he collapsed in a heap. A couple of cons who were passing dragged me off saying: 'For fuck sake, leave it out, Billy, you'll kill him.' I never expected any reprisals as there were only a couple of the Kray firm in the Hate Factory at the time and they were greatly outnumbered by Richardson's South London outfit.

The police had started their purge on all known organised crime and just before we were busted the Richardson gang had been busted. I had met Eddie Richardson a couple of times outside. We got on because, like me, he was the Krays' deadly enemy. In Wandsworth we would only ever have the chance to exchange a few words now and then as we were in separate wings. Frankie Fraser was in the hospital wing due to gunshot wounds in the leg and he walked with the aid of a walking stick. Working alongside me in the tailor's shop was a relative of Fraser by marriage called Brindle. We got on really well from the off and there was never a dull moment with him around.

I was really elated when one day whilst I was walking round the exercise yard (they call it an exercise yard but all you do for an hour is walk round two abreast in a huge gigantic circle) I spotted Chang a few yards in front of me. He was surprised and pleased to see me when I slipped up behind and tapped him on the shoulder. Of course we had a lot to talk about. He already knew that the bent copper was suspended, as he had been really fitted up, even more than me. The villain of the piece really was Whewell who was not a recognised member of our firm but desperately wanted to be.

I could see it was a pretty sore point with Chang so explained that the same thing had befallen me some time ago when I got six months for malicious damage committed by Chris Lambrianou, who had done more or less the same thing to try and impress me. I went on to tell Chang all the things that were going on outside. He was pleased we never went anywhere near the two girl witnesses as they were under a 24-hour surveillance and the only reason my bail was not objected to was that the police anticipated I would try to get to them and intimidate them so that they could do me for it. But we were all aware what they were up to. I spent all the daily exercises with Chang. Whewell was serving his five-year sentence in another prison, which was just as well – neither Chang nor I was too pleased about the situation we now found ourselves in.

Chang and I had heard that the bent copper had been charged with corruption and a *prima facie* case had been found against him. He had been committed to stand trial at the Old Bailey. I was pleased for Chang, as even though he was guilty his case had been blown up completely out of all proportion. Finally we were called up in front of the Prison Governor and told we would be attending the Old Bailey in connection with the copper's trial. I was, however, not too optimistic about him being convicted as all the evidence he was facing came from the criminal fraternity. My stepfather was called to relate a conversation he had witnessed in the copper's office, and my brother Ron, but he had a couple of petty convictions recorded against him for gaming so he was too tainted to be believed by the jury. The outcome was that the copper was acquitted but slung off the force.

To this day I feel the investigation team fell down on their job. They could have made a concrete case against him if, during his meeting with Ron, they had rigged him up with a bugging device or at least dusted the money they had given Ron to hand over for fingerprinting purposes. But this is history now and you must draw your own conclusions. At least we had rid the Metropolitan Police of one bad apple.

I was getting through the sentence pretty smoothly apart from being found in possession of a quantity of tobacco that was believed to have been smuggled in. I spent a few days in the chokey block, lost a few days' remission and had the tobacco confiscated. Towards the end of my sentence there was a strange little interlude when I was told to pack my kit as I was being shifted to Eastchurch Prison on the Isle of Sheppey. I had no say in the matter and was quite content to stay in the Hate Factory.

On arriving at Eastchurch Prison I never liked it at all and could not figure why they had decided to send me there. The following day I was called up in front of the Governor, who had my pile of prison records in front of him. Not one word was said to me whilst he was busy reading my file. I was a bit surprised at not being allocated a job. I was finally dismissed when he said, 'That will be all', and I made my way back to the kind of barrack-room which was to be my new residence.

It all reminded me very much of an army barracks and that brought back a lot of bad memories. It seemed I had the day to myself, so I wandered around the grounds. No one challenged me. I returned to the hut after a while. During the course of the day I had my lunch and tea and returned to my new residence.

After about an hour or so two screws entered the hut and approached me telling me to pack my kit. I never bothered to ask them what was happening as I don't suppose they would have enlightened me anyway. After I had packed my belongings I was escorted into a small brick building, placed in a cell and told I would be staying there overnight before being shipped back to Wandsworth in the morning. Obviously there had been some oversight by the Governor of Wandsworth or some official but I would never know. It was strange that I felt relieved to get back to the Hate Factory, which was so harsh, but at least I was back with Chang, Brindle, Tommy Harper and other friends of mine from the outside.

In Wandsworth I had other friends who are too numerous to mention whereas in Eastchurch Prison, although there was more freedom, I felt isolated amidst many strangers, some of whom were first-time offenders and alien to my way of life. In Wandsworth there was a lot of talk about Frank Mitchell's (the 'Mad Axeman') escape from Dartmoor Prison and it was a well-known fact the Krays were behind it. Then news started to filter in from newly convicted arrivals that Mitchell was now dead. These items of news were from reliable sources so the Kray image was even further tarnished – to many cons Mitchell, being so anti-establishment, was a cult figure and this latest development didn't sit well with them.

The Krays had been Frank's friends when he was inside, even to the extent of them paying for his defence when he was up for the attempted murder of another prisoner – and buying him a suit to wear in court. When he was convicted the twins visited him and kept him well supplied with money, and word was passed around the prison that he was a friend of the Krays and that anyone who forgot this did so at their peril. Mitchell always described the twins as 'the two best friends a man could have'.

No one really knows why the Krays arranged Mitchell's escape from Dartmoor. It was said that they needed him as one of their strong-arm men, but they had as many of these as they wanted. More than likely they got Mitchell out because since the murder of George Cornell, their contacts were steering clear and their business was suffering – life was getting uncomfortable for them. With their reputation going down, a helping hand to the underworld by springing a con out of Dartmoor would give a big boost to their prestige.

But Mitchell knew too much from the years he had spent in the company of members of the Kray gang and after his escape he became a threat to the Krays. He disappeared without trace, going off with them thinking they had arranged a weekend in the country for him with his girlfriend. No one knows exactly what happened to Frank Mitchell, and when the Krays and a gangster called Frederick Foreman were accused at the Old Bailey of murdering him, they were acquitted because the judge felt a conviction would be unsafe since all the evidence was from the criminal fraternity.

After I'd been back at Wandsworth for a month or so I was shifted to Pentonville Prison where I completed my sentence. When I got out I heard from various sources that the Kray firm was cracking up. Ronnie's bouts of madness were getting more frequent and his murder list was growing. All the old firm were slowly deserting and the Krays were replacing them with drifters such as the Lambrianous, whose youngest brother, Nicky, was being bedded by Ronnie Kray. They were also using the Lambrianous' parents' flat in East London to store their arsenal as Osborne's place had become too risky. Many of those wanting to leave the Krays' sinking ship were involved in some serious crime one way or the other, even murder, and living on their nerves, so the Krays made sure of implicating all their firm members in their crimes as a way of insurance of their allegiance. The Krays were desperate to find men with backbone and courage to replace some of the wimps who had taken over from the old gladiators who had been loyal until they saw with their own eyes that their leader was completely mad. Money was getting tighter for the Krays and they could no longer afford to foot the bill to have film stars and celebrities flown here from the States so that they could be seen wining and dining with them. No one with any sense got involved with them and they were living with their parents in a block of council flats in Bunhill Row.

Whilst I had been in the slammer my brother Ron had built things up, so much of the firm was still intact even though Chang's presence was missing. Betting offices were mushrooming but there were still illegal spielers in abundance and no shortage of cash coming in. At this time there was no pressure on us and we had no need to keep looking over our shoulder.

By this time too we were pretty legitimate in most of our dealings. I believe the police were a bit reluctant to cross swords with us owing to the police corruption trial, although if we were caught bang to rights breaking the law we were well aware that there would be no quarter given to us, nor could we expect any help from any member of the Metropolitan Police whatsoever.

The stories that have gone around about why Jack 'The Hat' McVitie was murdered by Reggie Kray have all missed the real beginnings of their differences. Reggie first met Jack in Wandsworth where McVitie was doing seven years for robbery and had just attacked the Governor and broken his jaw. Whenever I met McVitie he was out of his box on drugs and booze. He was always making threats against the Krays, especially against Ronnie, but I always considered them to be empty threats. What really began the trouble was when Jack acquired a lot of very valuable gold coins. One evening I was in a club called The Alphabet with my friend Chris Manning, when Jack 'The Hat' came in as high as a kite and penniless except for his coins which we didn't know about. He sat down with us and pulled out a handful of these gold coins. He said he had to meet some buyers for the coins at a club later on. He asked me and Chris and another guy named Terry if we would accompany him to look after him.

We all piled into McVitie's car and went to the meeting. While we were driving, Jack turned round to Chris in the back seat and said, 'What became of my pet rabbit you were looking after for me? I went to your house yesterday and the rabbit was gone.' Chris replied, 'Don't you remember, Jack, you strangled it the other night?' Jack just answered, 'Did I?'

It wasn't until we got near to the meeting that Jack told me it was the Krays who had heard about his coins and were anxious to buy them. I said to him, 'Forget it, Jack. They'll skin you alive and you'll be lucky to get a penny from them.' But he said, 'They'll never have me over' – meaning they'd pay up. I knew different but it was pointless trying to convince him.

When we arrived at the club, the doorman knew all four of us and when he saw Jack without a collar and tie he said, 'I can't let you in, Jack.' Jack said, 'Can't let me in? You're only the fucking boy!' Not wanting any nasty incident, the doorman said, 'Wait a minute and I'll get you something.' Within a minute or so he was back with a tie and told Jack to sit at the back of the club where it was darker and he wouldn't be so obvious. Within half an hour the Kray twins arrived with four of their firm and an appraiser of sorts.

Reggie said to me, 'Are you in on this, Billy?' I said, 'No, I'm a friend of Jack.' Jack had been popping pills in his mouth and was well into his second beer so by how he was high – a fully fledged space cadet. He never realised that they had brought an appraiser along to value his merchandise. Jack put a handful of coins on the table and the appraiser handled them and examined them for a minute or two then he nodded his head to the twins to show the coins were genuine.

Jack then said, 'Look, I'm fucking skint. There's nothing to eat indoors and I need some money real bad.' Reggie kept him in limbo for a few minutes and then said, 'I don't know the real value now and I haven't got much on me. I'll give you £40 now and the difference when we know the real value.' I could see they were having 'The Hat' over.

Even in the state he was in Jack realised that now the Krays had their hands on the coins they would not let go of them. Also he knew that the way things were going it would end up with a battle and we were greatly outnumbered. Besides which, it was sure that a couple of their firm were carrying some weapons for them. So Jack took the £40 from Reggie and the Krays went. After they'd gone, Jack said, 'That fucked them. I've kept four coins back' and he turned to Terry and said, 'Here's the tenner I owe you.'

We got back into Jack's car to return to The Alphabet but by now Jack was so high on booze and pills that he was missing cars by inches. He suggested that we go to another club for a drink but the erratic way he was driving made me think that if a police car spotted us we'd surely get a pull and, seeing as I was carrying a gun, I said, 'Forget it Jack, I've got to meet my brother in the Venus Rooms.' This was a club in Old Compton Street, Soho, which we were looking after.

Somehow we reached my car by The Alphabet and I left the three of them having a drink there while I went to meet my brother. At the meeting there was my brother, Dave Clare, the Walthamstow villain who had just joined our firm, and Willie Gregory, one of our pals from Glasgow. I told Ron about the meeting with McVitie and the Krays and he was furious, 'What the fucking hell's the matter with you. Don't you realise "The Hat" only wanted you and the others there to give him a bit of a back up against the Krays?' I said, 'I know, but I didn't think they'd turn up in such force.' Ron was feeling sorry for McVitie and said, 'Why the fuck didn't you do a deal with "The Hat"? You know what greedy bastards the twins are.'

'The Hat' never did get any more money for his coins and a couple of months later we heard that he was on their firm. Shortly after that we heard he was going round to the various clubs and establishments that they minded claiming that the Krays had sent him to collect the protection money. Many of the owners paid up, for Jack was often seen in their establishments in the Krays' company. Jack had realised that he had been ripped off with the coins and this was his way of recovering his loss. Also he was forever slagging them off and tarnishing their image – he had to be made an example of.

The outcome was that the Krays killed Jack 'The Hat'. I always got on well with McVitie. Some of his antics were really amusing, but sometimes he would go over the top and get stoned out of his box on purple hearts, black bombers and booze. He could be troublesome and would often walk into clubs and slag off the Krays. One of these times was when he got high on booze and black bombers and staggered into The Regency Club with a sawn-off shotgun threatening to shoot the twins. Of course this was soon reported back to the Krays. They decided he had gone too far and had worn out his usefulness. So the Krays decided that they would have to eliminate him. Jack 'The Hat' had dented their ego once too often.

It's a part of the Kray legend that Reggie Kray killed McVitie and that makes him some sort of a hero. That's how Reggie put it about but it wasn't like that. Lots of people say that the Krays are responsible for a lot more killings than they've been given credit for, but there's not one incident in their lives when the Krays have done one killing or chivving or beating on their own. Even when Ronnie Kray shot George Cornell he had Ian Barrie covering him with a shooter.

They didn't give Jack a chance, even though the target was one solitary person stoned out of his box on drugs and booze, incapable of standing, let alone fighting. The two Lambrianou brothers were sent to encourage 'The Hat' to an early grave. He was lured with the promise of booze and birds. There were eight men involved in killing him – the Lambrianous, two brothers by the name of Mills, the twins' cousin, Ronnie Hart, a member of the Kray firm called Ronnie Bender and the Krays. Worst of the lot were the Lambrianou brothers who claimed that Jack was a friend of theirs. When 'The Hat' tried to run it took nearly everyone in the room to hold him back. In the end Ronnie held him in an arm lock while Reggie stabbed him in the face and the stomach and then nailed him to the floor through his throat. Then a minute after Jack had been butchered to death, Chris Lambrianou sat down on the stairs sobbing his heart out for his 'friend'. What a state the Lambrianous' souls must be in to be bought so cheaply! Their 'fee' for doing what they did was acceptance into the Kray firm.

Ronnie Kray always maintains McVitie was out to kill him and that 'The Hat' was scum and deserved to die. But just about anyone who was around at the time knows what happened. The real reason he got murdered was that he was making the Krays look foolish. I'm not saying that 'The Hat' was not a tainted person. He was an out and out villain, usually under the influence of booze and drugs, and could be a bit nasty. But he was not without friends so he couldn't have been all that bad. Sadly, there is no one to speak up for poor McVitie now as everyone is caught up in this Kray mania. It was the McVitie murder that did for the Krays and most of their mob. Ronnie got life imprisonment with a recommendation that he does at least 30 years for the murders of McVitie and George Cornell, and Reggie got the same for the McVitie murder. The Lambrianou brothers both got 15 years for being implicated in the murder of McVitie, and the Krays' brother, Charlie, was convicted of disposing of McVitie's body and got ten years for it. Of course he denied it and he still does.

McVitie's body was never found although there were plenty of rumours circulating through the East End – that it was concreted in the foundations of a building in the City, or it was made into pig food, or it was put into the furnace of Bankside Power Station. Another theory was that the twins had got a local undertaker to get rid of it. There were always stories in the East End that the twins paid privately for some cremations. Some say it is possible to put an additional body in an occupied coffin before the lid is screwed down.

Whilst things were going better than ever for us the Kray empire was beginning to totter and crumble. Many of the old faces on their firm had become disenchanted and were looking for ways out of their predicament. A few of them approached us and would have an occasional drink with us. Through one of them we heard that the Krays had a small factory near Romford, Essex, which was manufacturing purple hearts. Ronnie Kray was getting more paranoid than ever and the list in the book in which he would write the names of people he wanted to kill was growing in length. The pair of them were taking pills by the handful and were constantly turning on members of their own firm. Ronnie Kray still had his small army of young boys who would be bedded by him and act as his spies at the same time. There were always people who didn't know the full extent of the Krays' activities and so were eager to get on the Kray firm.

CHAPTER THIRTEEN

The Battle of the Old Horns

At about this time we were looking after a fella who was the main man in smuggling pornography into the country from Denmark. His was a big operation and he brought the goods into the country by the container-load. He also smuggled hand-guns by putting them in the same container. This was safe for us as we were not directly involved in the smuggling activities or the distribution and selling. We just kept people off his back and were paid handsomely for our protection and for making things run smoothly. It was not money I was proud of, but if we had not been part of the operation, others would.

The Krays had an inkling of what was going on and, seeing it was so lucrative, they wanted to muscle in. As could be expected, I would not allow this. Inevitably a quarrel started as Ronnie Kray assumed I could be persuaded into taking them in as partners. This could not be achieved and a war started. It began when we received an invitation to meet the twins and talk about the business.

Many times we had got word that they were anxious to have a meeting with us. Ron and I discussed the possibility of a meeting with the Krays many times but Ron was against it and I, whilst I was not too keen, was a bit curious. One of the last times I had seen Reggie was when I was having a visit in Wandsworth Prison and he was visiting his friend, Ossie. Their visit ended before mine and before leaving the visiting room he approached me and asked how I was keeping. He was pleasant enough and I spent a few moments with him before he left and I was able to resume my visit.

Although my brother Ron and I found it hard to tolerate Ronnie Kray with his domineering ways, we eventually decided we would have a meeting with the twins and hear what they had to say. It was set up in the Old Horns public house in Bethnal Green – a Kray stronghold where they and all their friends congregated.

We arrived at the pub with a couple of friends who were just ordinary working-class fellas we had been having a meal with earlier on. One of them was a fella called Ian who knew the Richardsons. When we entered the pub all the Kray firm were there in force, including a couple with whom I'd had several rows and arguments in the past. One was a fella by the name of Checker Berry who was married to Beryl Parkes, an ex-girlfriend of my brother Ron. Berry had been an associate of the Krays since they were at school and after Ronnie was certified insane during a period in Winchester Gaol, Berry would take him to stay in the country with farming friends to get out of things for a while. There was no love lost between me and Checker.

As we entered Ronnie Kray was sitting at the bar talking to Nicky, the youngest of the Lambrianou brothers, who was about 20 and young enough to attract Ronnie. The pub was practically packed solid but I noticed Scotch Jack Dickson, the one-time safe blower, Big Albert Donaghue, Tommy Cowley, the ginger-headed gambler, and Chrissie and Tony Lambrianou. To us this was just a meeting but although we were prepared for trouble I knew Chrissie and Tony would not get involved as their bottle had well and truly gone over their reluctant involvement in killing Jack 'The Hat'. But there were plenty of others who would want to find favour in the Krays' eyes.

When Ronnie Kray saw Ron and me and our friends enter he ordered us a drink and started the conversation by saying he had heard lots of reports that we were doing well. Then Reggie joined us and said he had heard I was out of the nick some time ago. He asked who our friends were and I introduced them to him. Ronnie Kray then called me aside and told me he would have preferred that Ron and I had come alone as they had some personal things to discuss with us. By now I was getting the impression that he knew more about our operations than I had imagined and that he had it in for me and Ron that night.

Whilst Ronnie Kray was talking to me I looked round to see where my brother Ron had got to and as I glanced around the pub I noticed most of the Krays' old firm were nowhere to be seen. I knew The Bear had recently got out as he had been wise enough to sever any involvement with them. Ronnie Kray then went on to ask if we needed any muscle now that Chang was away. I realised that he was trying to worm his way into our comparatively safe operation, so I told him we had everything more or less sewn up. Suddenly he changed the subject and asked me how my family were – and there was a bit of menace creeping into his voice. Again he asked me what I thought of one or two of his men helping me and Ron out, to which I replied, 'No, everything's under control.' He was aware that I had been a friend of Cornell's and that the Richardsons had been in Wandsworth along with me. He then went on about the Richardsons getting sent down and the amount of time they got. After that he said he knew Cornell was in my company on the day he got killed. By then he was showing all the Ronnie Kray danger signs. His voice had become almost a whisper and his eyes had begun to bulge.

I began to realise that because he wasn't getting a foot in the door with our various rackets he was looking for an excuse to have a battle right there and then, and this wasn't to our liking as we were outnumbered by about 20 to one. I thought I noticed as he was talking to me that he was motioning to members of his firm with his eyes. I was aware that many of his firm would relish the thought of having a dig at me and Ron, especially Checker Berry, who would enjoy the chance of putting one on to us. Ronnie then asked me what I thought about the Richardsons' sentence and I replied, 'I think they got a bad result. Charlie Richardson didn't merit getting 25 years'. To which he said, 'Well it won't happen to us as we've got too much help!'

Then suddenly he threw a punch which I anticipated and blocked. I threw a shot back at his chin which caught him on the forehead, and all hell broke loose. Young Nicky Lambrianou tried to get out of the action and our two friends were not fighting men and had the sense to stand well clear. Fortunately Scotch Jack Dickson and a couple of the others who have always been on good terms with us never threw a punch and remained neutral. The Lambrianous stayed on the sidelines.

I looked around for my brother and I was fully aware that we were in for a battle for survival and had to keep our feet – if we hit the floor we would be killed where we dropped. Little ginger-haired Tommy Cowley came at my brother with a blade but Ron hurled a stool at him. Thank God we had just had the one drink or things would have been much worse. Ron fought his way towards me and together, standing back to back, we managed to make our way out of the door without losing our footing. We gave nearly as much as we got but we were so overwhelmed we took a lot of punishment before, thankfully, we were able to make good our escape. Later I was told that one of the twins had a shooter on him that night but had second thoughts about using it on us.

I had several cuts and wounds but Ron's wounds were much worse than mine. Can you imagine the feeling of escaping from the clutches of a homicidal maniac and his twin brother out of their minds on drugs and booze, not to mention their firm, many of whom wanted a piece of revenge? As well as being on the Kray firm, for some of them it was a personal matter – over the years I have pulled occasional strokes on several people. I am sure to this day if Ron and I hadn't kept on our feet and battled together to get out of the building we would now both be nothing but another chapter in a book about the Krays. And as it is I am sure beyond all doubt that my brother, whom I was so close to, would be alive today if it had not been for the beating he took that day in the Old Horns.

When we got through the doors it was pouring with rain – and blood was streaming down our faces from the numerous head wounds we had received. When you are being attacked in a crowd situation like that it's your head and hands that take the most punishment. Our pocket handkerchiefs were soaking wet with a mixture of blood and rain. We had no headwear and I could feel the rain pelting down into my head wounds. We made our way to the casualty department of the children's hospital in Hackney Road. The staff nurse thought we were a couple of drunks who'd got into a fight and was so rude and treated us with such disdain we walked out and made our way to St Leonard's hospital in Kingsland Road. We tried getting a cab there but they were all occupied. Every time we heard a cab behind us we thought it was a Kray car searching for us, but eventually we reached the hospital where the sister was more humane. She wanted us to stay overnight for observation but we decided against it. We were well aware that the Krays had killed many people and others had disappeared, and we knew we were not immune and they might start searching for us in local hospitals. Then we had our wounds cleaned and stitched and a finger on my left hand X-rayed. I found out it was broken and to this day it is still crooked and practically useless. Ron had many more injuries than me – if I had not had him at my side I would surely have been yet another one of the Krays' corpses.

I revisited the hospital a few times for some therapeutic treatment to try and straighten my finger but it never worked. Ron's injuries were so much worse than mine and he never fully recovered, suffering worse and worse headaches right up to his death. Since that night the hatred I feel towards Ronnie Kray is indescribable. He is never out of my mind. Until then I had never known how hate can be so consuming that all you can think of is revenge. To be so full of hate and bitterness is a terrible thing. I would pray to God to show me the way. Clergymen and men of God would tell me to forgive and forget. God! I wish I could.

I know now that there were several reasons for the Krays to set up the meeting with us at the Old Horns. One was that Ronnie Kray was determined to get into my lucrative set-up. Another reason was that the Krays knew the net was closing in and they were trying to make sure that in the event of Old Bill questioning anyone who had had dealings with them in the past and had been shot, stabbed or maimed, their victims would not talk to the police. But when things don't go to plan with Ronnie Kray, all his reasons go up in smoke. The incident in the Old Horns happened just a couple of weeks before they were arrested. Although they were in the Horns that night, Big Albert Donaghue and Scotch Jack Dickson took no part in the battle as they were friends of ours. Of course they could not intervene on our side as the Krays and the rest of the mob would have turned on them. So Scotch Jack and Big Albert remained friends of ours after the battle. I found out since that Reggie was armed with a gun that night and he could have killed Ron and me as cold-bloodedly as he killed Jack 'The Hat' and his brother killed George Cornell.

The Krays had by now become important enough for the police to set up a special unit to try and get enough on them to put them off the streets altogether. Nipper Read's team was operating from Tintagel House, a large block of government offices on the other side of the river. It wasn't long before Ron and I were taken there to be questioned about the Krays. Believe me, there is no honour whatsoever amongst thieves or villains when one's flesh and blood is battered to a pulp by a raving homosexual and his gang of hangers-on – who, apart from the odd few, were a threat to no one.

My hatred of the twins was so much that I readily told Detective Inspector Mooney, a genial Irishman, and his colleagues all about the night in the Old Horns. I made a statement about a raving, demented lunatic. Unashamedly, I wished the thought had entered my mind before to blow the whistle on the Krays, then they would have been off the streets sooner. There was no pressure put on us to make the statements that are on file, nor was there any deal made with Nipper Read, Inspector Mooney or any of the Kray gangbusters. Until now nobody knows of the existence of the statements we made apart from those we dictated them to.

By now the cracks in the Kray empire could be seen. After Cornell was killed the Krays' business began to fall off. Some West End clubs they were minding decided they were too dangerous to know and made other arrangements. One top gambling club gave them £10,000 to end their contract. The pity was that at this time none of their firm had the bottle to blow the whistle on them although they wanted to.

It took three women to stand up to them after they killed George Cornell. One was George's wife, Olive, who always knew who killed him. She did everything she could to undermine the twins and even threw a brick through the window of the Kray family home in Vallance Road, Bethnal Green. The twins' mother Violet, came out and when Olive Cornell called her sons murderers, she burst into tears and said her boys would never do anything like that.

The barmaid in the Blind Beggar who saw the shooting went to the police in the end and said she wanted to tell the truth, although she was under threat to keep quiet. The other woman who shopped them was Carol Skinner, whose flat was used to kill Jack 'The Hat' McVitie. Although she didn't know it, Ronnie Kray had already decided that she'd have to be killed and told one of his firm that he'd hired a woman assassin to kill her.

The twins were certain that some ex-members of their firm were talking to the police and they were beginning to see the writing on the wall after the killing of Cornell. They fled the country to Tangiers for three weeks and there they saw a lot of Billy Hill. Maybe they could see the sense of retiring like he had but they didn't seem able to make a decision to get right out. They stepped up their reign of terror and anyone they thought was going to leave the firm got a dead rat through the post or a wreath delivered to his house. They'd always kept their firm together with fear, not loyalty. As one of their firm said at their trial, 'When Ronnie tells you to do something, you do it or get shot yourself.'

Then they were arrested. I was in The Pegasus and Scotch Jack Dickson broke the news to me. It was Scotch Jack and Ian Barrie who went with Ronnie to the Blind Beggar to murder George Cornell. I was over the moon at the news of the twins being nicked, although at the time I do not think I had much hatred for Reggie. It was all festering and directed at his twin brother.

I think more than anything I despised Reggie for never ever taking a stand against his evil brother's total domination. Maybe if he had, many people would be alive today and their kinsfolk would still be with their loved ones. Night after night I would lie in my bed thinking of revenge and many, many things entered my mind. The 30 years' sentence the Krays subsequently finished up with meant little to me, but the revenge I craved for so much would come to me in a way I'd not anticipated.

There's a lot of talk about loyalty among the members of the Kray firm. When the crunch came none of them were what you would call well-off. All the mob members were getting was £30 a week plus free drinks, and for this they had to be totally loyal. The Krays always boasted that members of their firm gave them total allegiance. What this meant was that if by chance someone on their firm did not participate in a fight the Krays would see to it that after the battle the rest of them would turn on him and give him an unmerciful kicking. That's how they achieved total allegiance. But believe me, when the Kray firm saw which way the wind was blowing they soon began to desert the sinking ship. This made Ronnie absolutely paranoid and he turned on everyone. He firmly believed they were all conspiring against him. And some of them were. Their cousin, Ronnie Hart, who'd helped them get rid of the body of Jack 'The Hat' turned Queen's evidence in the end. Their old business partner, Leslie Payne, made a statement to Nipper Read when he heard he was on Ronnie's murder list and Scotch Jack Dickson also talked to the law. People had had enough, no matter what their relationship with the Krays was. There was relief that they were off the streets.

During the next couple of years I met many villains and thieves who had been themselves victims of the Kray firm. Each and every one was greatly outnumbered by the Kray firm, and lured into traps set up by the twins. Thieves were relieved of their stolen merchandise and straight businessmen's lives were in ruins – many contemplated suicide. The misery the Krays brought was widespread and each and every villain I spoke to would dearly love the chance to get Ronnie Kray on his own in a room. But now he was safely under lock and key.

From then on it was business as usual with all the rackets that will always go on in London – the spielers, the protection firms who keep the peace, not break it, the drinking clubs – all went on without the threat of the Krays getting involved or wanting a piece of the take with the usual bloodshed and without the extra activities of the police who followed the twins wherever they went.

In spite of all this you can turn on the television and see ordinary people from the East End saying what a good thing it would be if the twins were to be released. That they are really a kind and loving pair always giving to charity and are greatly missed. This is rubbish and does not take into consideration the reality of what they did and the fear it inspired in everyone when they were on the streets.

I sincerely hope that in the event of the Krays reading this it adds salt to their wounds. They say there is a code in the criminal world that it is wrong to make statements to the police, but when you see a loved one taking a beating so terrible that he never fully recovers, all you want is revenge. You become consumed with hatred and all the so-called criminal codes of conduct amount to nothing. I eventually finished up nursing my hatred but always felt that somehow, some way, I will get the opportunity so that whatever is covered up will be uncovered.

I never had any business dealings with their elder brother Charlie but whilst the twins were at liberty I would see quite a lot of him and his wife Dolly, and I remember his young son Gary when he was a very young schoolboy, aged about seven or eight, who constantly wore a patch over one of his eyes. He always seemed a quiet, shy boy but very likeable. The last time I saw him he was working for one of the national newspapers as a van boy delivering newspapers to the shops from the printing works.

Now at least, with the Krays out of the way, London's underworld was not under so much scrutiny and all the hangers-on disappeared off the face of the earth – or maybe they crawled back into their holes. It seemed to prove how they had been like the centre of a sore which just festered and grew, and when the centre was removed it all disappeared.

Chang by now had been released and it was good to have him back. We were spending a lot of time in Edmonton, as in the mid-Sixties, we had really become good friends with many people from that area, many of whom are firm friends to this present day. It was through one of Chang's many deals I got to know Vera Manning who originated from Ireland and had a strong Irish accent. At the time her husband Chris was in the slammer doing a couple of years. He was a pretty good thief and had done quite a bit of villainy with Jack 'The Hat' McVitie.

At the time Vera was living in Church Street and night or day her door was always open to us. She knew practically everyone worth knowing – the only problem was that she was always high on something or other and liked the booze, as did Chris. Vera's younger sister Marie was a hooker who used the Glenrae hotel. Marie was found dead in the bath, the cause of death being electrocution. An electric fire was found in the bath. At the inquest an open verdict was recorded. Vera maintains the Krays were involved in some way, but this may be just talk, although I can't see any reason otherwise for Vera to make this accusation. Maybe Marie upset them as, like Vera, she was almost habitually on drugs and into crooked deals. But I think Marie's death was after the Krays were put in the slammer, so I don't put much credence on what I've been told anyway.

I've always believed the Krays knew more about the death of Freddie Mills, the fighter who, it was alleged, shot himself in his car in 1965. I never bought the idea that he took his own life, nor did his family who believed he was murdered. There are still programmes on television from time to time pointing out that it would have been impossible for him to have done so given the position the rifle was in. Once again the Krays were lurking in the wings and paying him a visit in his nightclub in Charing Cross Road. This was when the Krays were trying to muscle in on his club with threats of violence and blackmail. Shortly after that one of the Sunday nationals published an article stating that Freddie Mill's Nitespot was a place of disrepute used by hookers. All this reeks of the Kray *modus operandi*. Within a year Freddie was dead. Around that time the Krays had just beaten extortion charges and the Old Bill were a bit wary to go near them.

People in the know will never forgive the Krays for what happened to Frank Mitchell, whom they blasted out of Dartmoor

Prison and then disposed of. It's obvious what happened to him, along with many others. However, the Kray propaganda machine can and will get the gullible public to believe anything. To this day Ronnie Kray claims that Frank underwent plastic surgery and is living abroad. How can anyone go along with Ronnie Kray's claim that Mitchell is now in a foreign country? How could a man with his child-like mentality possibly remain hidden for over 25 years? Yet Ronnie Kray still says that one day Mitchell will emerge. Anyone that goes along with that must be besotted by the Krays. Nipper Read has said on television that he investigated seven murders whilst he was after the Krays. Draw your own conclusions.

CHAPTER FOURTEEN

Visiting the Twins

In 1969, some time after the Krays were tried and convicted, my brother Ron and I appeared in front of the Criminal Injuries Compensation Board because of the permanent damage which had been done to us at the Old Horns. People of my calibre are viewed in an entirely different light than people from the straight world, so we were not disappointed or disillusioned when we were not awarded a penny compensation, as from our early childhood days whatever happened we were always seen as the aggressors, never the victims. If we retaliated and handed out a few cuts and bruises to the instigators or antagonists, we were always the villains of the piece. So the knock back from the Criminal Injuries Compensation Board did not surprise us.

I know it was said that we should not have complained to the Criminal Injuries Board because there is a code of conduct in the criminal world that it is wrong to make statements to the police. But when I had seen my brother taking a beating so terrible that he never fully recovered, all I wanted was revenge. I was eaten up with hatred – all the so-called criminal codes of conduct amounted to nothing.

After the Krays were put away there was a change in London. There was less organised crime but more general violence and bad behaviour, which made our services in protection even more necessary. The Kray firm would have capitalised on this kind of violence at the cost of more and terrible bloodshed.

I was still having an occasional drink or meal in the West End, though I am not and never have been a heavy drinker. I don't know why this should be, as much of my time is spent in clubs, so people are a bit shocked when I'm offered a drink and I opt for a tonic water or orange juice. One evening in 1971 when Chang and I were in the West End just after midnight, I called into the Venus Rooms in Soho on the chance of seeing an old friend who often frequented the club.

We were sitting at the bar having a casual conversation with the barman. I recall it was a weekday and pretty quiet as it was quite early also. We were just thinking about leaving as the meeting with this pal of mine was not too important, when we were approached by a guy whose face was vaguely known to me. For the moment it just didn't register although he seemed to know me well enough. He told me he had been hoping I would be in the Venus Rooms. He was very sociable and said he would like a word with me. There was nothing unusual in this so I suggested he sit down with Chang and me. The guy asked us what we were drinking and ordered. After the waiter had brought the drinks to the table we sat back to hear what he had to say.

He started straight in by telling us that the twins were now together in Parkhurst. He was not very subtle at the offset and both I and Chang were riled up. By now Chang was all ready to give him a shot. I stood up saying, 'Are you fucking trying to dig me out?' To which he went deathly white and said, 'Listen, listen! Hear me out.' Chang said, 'Who the fucking hell are you and what do you want?' He said, 'Please at least hear me out – you've got nothing to lose and a lot to gain.' He then resumed the conversation which had calmed down by now by saying Reggie Kray wanted to see me. To which I replied, 'Is he fucking mad or what? He's in maximum security.'

I couldn't make head nor tail of any of this coming right out of the blue. I kept trying to fathom him out but I could make no sense of it whatsoever. The more I pondered this bombshell that had been landed in my lap the more confused it all became. We sat in silence for a couple of minutes then Chang said, 'I can't see why Reggie couldn't have got a stiff (smuggled uncensored letter) out to Billy.' To which he replied, 'Some of the things are personal.' I replied, 'Why me?' All this cloak and dagger stuff did not sit well with me so I said, 'What does he suggest I do? Break in the prison?' To which he replied, 'As I said before, you've got nothing to lose but much to gain.'

By now I was beginning to fathom things out a little. I was aware, as were many others, that the Krays had tucked some money away, but it could be numerous other things. I asked him if he had visited Reggie, to which he replied, 'No, but I visit Charlie.' So I said, 'Well what exactly does he expect?' To which he replied, 'It's best he tells you that. Maybe you could get a one-off visit.' Chang then broke in by saying, 'Well, let Billy give it some thought and then get in touch with you in a week's time. They won't be going anywhere just yet.' To which the fella replied, 'That's fine', and wrote a phone number down on a piece of paper.

Whilst Chang and I were driving home we tried to make some sense out of all that had gone on in the Venus Rooms. Chang said, 'Maybe there's a pot of gold at the end of this rainbow.' At this early stage so many things entered my mind that nothing was ruled out. I even thought the Krays were trying to involve me in some way – I knew from first-hand experience they were no amateurs in putting people in the frame. It was so hard to speculate on something of which we knew so little. The face of the stranger was familiar and now I realised I should have asked him where I'd met him before but the opportunity had long gone. By now I wanted to go and sort this turn of events over in my mind, as well as talk to Ron about it.

Chang and I drove to Stamford Hill to Johnny Stock's all-night cafe, where we were hoping we might find Ron. On arriving there we spotted Ron with Johnny 'The Eyes' Gardner, who had been on our firm more or less from its beginnings. With him was Wally

'The Map' Gore, another tried and trusted friend. Johnny Stock's cafe was a spacious place, so although it was quite crowded we could speak with some privacy. When I told Ron all that had gone on earlier that evening in the Venus Rooms he was as astounded as I was. After discussing the situation for some time we decided that there might be a lot of money in sight as we were well aware that during the Krays' reign they had accumulated a lot of wealth.

After a couple of days in which I often found myself pondering over this strange request from Reggie Kray I realised it was not so strange, as even in our early days when we were fellow deserters from the army he would confide in me and talk about his problems, and more often than not he would go along with what I suggested. So now all this began to make sense. The guy we had met in the Venus Rooms was duly phoned up a couple of days later and told that I would set the wheels in motion to visit Reggie Kray in Parkhurst Prison. Perhaps at the back of my mind I could see ways to both earn from keeping them in and at the same time get my own back.

In those early years only visitors approved by the Home Office prior to a visit from the local police to the applicant's home were allowed permission to visit a maximum security prisoner. I heard that even a magistrate was refused from the list of approved visitors. A couple of days later I penned a letter to the Home Office saying I was emigrating to Australia with my family (by now I was married with a young son and daughter) and before I left England I would like to be granted a special visit to my friends the Kray twins. I cannot remember the letter in its entirety but as diabolical as it was in content it got the right result. Shortly after it was despatched I got a reply from the Home Office stating that after giving the matter some consideration it was decided a visit would be granted. I was surprised at this as it would have been a simple matter for the Home Office to have checked up and found there was no record or any sign to suggest that I had any intention of emigrating – and what country would accept me?

Surely they must have known that I had made a statement about various incidents in connection with the twins to Inspector Mooney of the murder squad and that I hated them. So this was highly suspicious to me – it would have been easier for the Home Office to have refused the visit. What I mean is, why was I allowed to enter a maximum security prison designed solely to keep people like me out?

I told Ron that the visit had been granted and I would be taking my wife and daughter Debbie, who was then five years old. This was because I had told the Home Office in my letter that I was taking my family on the visit and I believe this was the stipulation laid down for the visit.

A week or so later Debbie, my wife and I found ourselves in the maximum security block of Parkhurst Prison. When we got there I felt certain that the room would be bugged, and to this day nothing will make me believe otherwise. I won't buy the idea that the Home Office granted the visit for reasons of compassion, reasonableness or consideration. Shortly after we had been seated awaiting the arrival of Reggie he appeared, but to my surprise he was accompanied by his twin brother Ronnie. I never expected his presence and he must have seen my hostile expression when I looked in his eyes. It was obvious Ronnie was heavily sedated as I know all the signs – I myself have often been a user of various pills to keep me awake and alert during long gaming sessions.

I felt nothing but hatred for this man although I did feel some compassion for Reggie. I realised that with the bugging I would have to be selective about anything I spoke about. I signalled to make Reggie aware of this situation and he understood.

Reggie went on to tell me that many people were in their debt and much money was owing to them. He told me the money was owed by a number of establishments that he and his twin were still minding and he wanted me to arrange collection. They were places that I knew well so this caused no problems as the people who ran them knew me. All during the visit Ronnie Kray never said a word, which must have been extremely difficult for him as he was always at the head of everything in the past and here he was taking a back seat.

After talking to me about business, Reggie talked a bit to my daughter Debbie. He must have liked her at first sight, for after that he spoke about his mother, Violet Kray, and said that she would like to meet me again and that she would also like to meet Debbie. He then suggested that the next time his mother visited him, she would bring Debbie with her. He told me that Violet always visited the twins on a Saturday, so I arranged with Reggie to take my daughter to his mother's flat on Saturday morning. Reggie then told me his parents were practically the only visitors they ever had. I replied I would drop in on them when I was in the vicinity and with that the visit came to an end.

Soon after my visit to Reggie in Parkhurst, I took Debbie to meet the twins' mother, Violet, and she was very pleased. She was fond of children and made a fuss of Debbie. Likewise Debbie came to be very fond of Violet. The twins' father was also at the flat. So it was arranged that Debbie went with Violet on her next visit to the Krays. This arrangement went on for many years. I knew Reggie was forming an interest of some kind in her because he always mentioned her in his letters to me. After one of her visits he wrote, 'I am pleased that Debbie goes to church.' Considering the fact that his letters to me were always of a business nature, it was hard for me to believe that he had been struck with religion.

Debbie and I were genuinely fond of Violet, the more so Debbie as she would often stay at the flat prior to the train journey to Portsmouth and the sea crossing by ferry to the Isle of Wight. Week after week, Violet would make her journey with Debbie to Parkhurst Prison and visit the Krays. Debbie really looked forward to these outings, especially the trip on the ferry. Even after Violet died, Debbie still carried on visiting Reggie over the years and there was always a car laid on for her paid for with Kray money. The visits started when Debbie was six and ended when she was a young woman. After one of these visits he said to her in a letter, 'You look smart and beautiful. Write out your measurements for me.' And when the visits stopped, he continued writing to her and his letters became more and more intimate. In one letter from Gartree Prison he wrote, 'I'm not tied up with anyone romantically, are you?' And besides sending Debbie a picture of himself with Billy Hill, once known as 'King of the Underworld', he also sent her Valentine cards. I want to make it quite clear that my daughter never had any romantic interest in Reggie Kray, and it was only the circumstances of her meeting him as a small child which led her into a relationship of any kind with him, although it was obvious that Reggie was seeing her as someone who would be there for him when he finally came out of prison. In one of his letters to her he says, 'We could go on a world tour for three months.' Obviously Debbie felt compassion for him but she had no designs on him and certainly no intention of going on any cruise on his release.

Now that we had business to do together Reggie and I also kept in contact by prison letters, though all of these were censored – matters of a personal nature came via a stiff smuggled out of the prison by Violet or by verbal personal messages. My feelings were a bit confused and mixed towards him. He was complex to say the least.

After my first visit to Reggie in Parkhurst I told Ron all that had transpired. What Reggie had suggested seemed lucrative providing we were subtle and made no open threats. We decided we must be reasonable, not greedy like the Krays in their unreasonableness and lust for power.

After a lot of discussion on the proposition Reggie had put to me we decided to go ahead. We decided we were going to be a bit selective about what clubs we would take on. Some, we felt, were not worth considering for various reasons. The main reason was that however subtle our approach to the proprietors, they could quite easily blow the whistle on us and we would finish up like the Krays – as 'Her Majesty's guests'. Meetings were made with the various club owners whose main priority was that no disturbance was perpetrated in their clubs and that undesirables were kept out of their establishments.

So a scam was set in operation. The registered office was supposed to be at brother Ron's address in Epsom, Surrey. The East London premises were at relations of mine in Hackney Road the West London office was an accommodation address in Mayfair. We had business cards and stationery printed as Double R Enterprises, the Double R standing for Reggie and Ronnie, suggesting the Kray organisation was still operating. The stationery was headed S. Houston and W. Webb (that was me), the supposed directors. Various establishments were approached and undertakings promised. Of course Chang came in with us. He was very creditable so no one thought otherwise. Of course we made sure that none of the places we approached were in any way connected with Billy Hill, who although he had long retired was still in contact with places he had minded, like Churchill's which he had handed over to the Krays. What we offered in those early days was a straightforward deal with maybe just a subtle hint of menace. Our service was more or less on a par with the security guards that are in operation in this present day and age.

Being a reasonable man, I easily got a foot in the door of the most vulnerable clubs. I made it quite clear that I had no intention of monopolising any establishment nor was I expecting a percentage of their profits, at least not from the legally licensed gambling and drinking clubs. The unlicensed ones were a different matter altogether. There was still plenty I did not know about the Kray organisation, but due to the circumstances of our meeting I could not draw anything at all out of Reggie. Rightly or wrongly, we decided that we did not have to hand over any of the money we collected to Reggie Kray.

But however we handled the money, both the Krays were grateful to me for linking them with the outside world and from then on I received regular letters from both of them which went on until 1990. They even sent me two paintings done by them in Parkhurst Prison. One is a picture of Christ hanging on the cross and the other is a landscape. They are very crude and bear no comparison to the paintings done by my brother Ron, which show real artistic talent.

CHAPTER FIFTEEN

'Can You Get Me a Boy?'

In the mid-Seventies my Uncles Alf and Bob retired from the sawdust factory started by my grandfather and were anxious for me to take it over. But my knowledge of the sawdust business was non-existent and although it was a family business it was an alien way of life to me. I decided I would take the business over and bought my uncles out on the understanding that I had no intention of carrying on the old-established business as I had other plans in mind. Soon a deal was settled and the cash handed over.

The building was a three-storey affair with a shop front and a basement situated in Hackney Road on the corner of Dinmont Street. Soon I hired casual labour to convert it into a gambling and drinking club (unlicensed of course) and as a front for other businesses. One of my contacts acquired damaged, shop-soiled and other miscellaneous items, all bought for next to nothing, and we sold them on to the public cheaply. The shop was in the heart of the East End and there was no shortage of customers. The shop was useful as it doubled as a front for the gambling club which was at the back of the building. The premises also had a large forecourt that I rented out to a friend of mine who was a car dealer – we worked that on a percentage basis. The cars were sold at a fast and furious rate as we were situated directly on Hackney Road, but like all good things it never lasted long. The local council soon got word of what I was doing with the forecourt and wrote several letters telling me to stop. For ages I led them a song and dance but carried on trading as they were unable to serve a summons. Finally, after much perseverance, they obtained an injunction. But my pal still put the occasional car up for sale in front of the shop. Eventually the council erected concrete bollards on the forecourt and this finished the car business. However, the spieler and drinking club went on thriving.

Finally we had a bit of a set-back as the friend who was running the shop put some stolen dresses on one of the rails on the forecourt and the local Old Bill paid a visit and took the stolen dresses away. I was phoned up and told of the incident and subsequently appeared at the local court charged with receiving stolen goods. Fortunately I had a pretty good solicitor and the law never verballed me up, thinking they had a cast-iron case.

I eventually appeared in front of the magistrates at Old Street Magistrates Court where I strenuously denied the charge. In spite of my villainous-looking scars I dressed very conservatively, as I imagined the run-of-the-mill shopkeeper would dress. At one point I even thought of putting a money apron on, but this would be going a bit too far. So I decided on just an off-the-peg suit. I felt a bit of a burk really as I am normally a smart dresser.

After my solicitor had said his piece I entered the witness box all ready. I explained to the magistrates that I had bought the goods from a woman who had told me that she owned a small clothing factory nearby and who had said that the dresses were made up from the material that was left over from some big orders she had received from the trade. In the dress trade these items are called 'cabbage'. I went on to say that if I had any idea the dresses were stolen I was hardly likely to put them on the forecourt for all the world to see. After a short consideration the magistrate acquitted me, but specified that I was to receive no court costs and would have none of my legal fees refunded. Of course I was delighted at being given what the magistrate termed 'the benefit of the doubt'.

Fortunately the local Old Bill merely took the dresses away and never searched my premises, so I was able to carry on with the gambling and drinking club. No doubt the arresting officers were a bit peeved but maybe I was so convincing in the witness box that they too were taken in – they certainly didn't appear too bright. I'm sure they would have had a hell of a surprise if they had searched the building. We were open practically 24 hours a day as word soon gets round to the ardent gamblers. I continued like this for a number of years and despite a few small skirmishes things went smoothly.

Many villains, thieves and the odd confidence trickster would be among our clientele. Some of the guys from South London who were pretty big gamblers were habitual users of the club. The boxer Buller Ward often dropped in. He was one of the many whose hatred of Ronnie Kray was absolute, like the many thieves who had risked their liberty to acquire stolen goods and then in turn had them stolen off them by the Krays.

In 1975 the Krays' elder brother, Charlie, was released. Shortly after this Ron and I were invited to attend a private party to celebrate his release at a club near Liverpool Street in the City. Ron declined but I went along. It was a pretty smart do and a pretty formal affair. When I sat at the table I found I was directly opposite Tommy Cowley, who was one of the Kray mob who had set on Ron and me in the Old Horns.

When he saw me he started wishing he had not come. He didn't have a mob with him now and was so nervous that he was shaking. He tried a sickly smile but I looked right through him. Then he had the cheek to ask how Ron was and I replied, 'He should be here shortly.' When I said this all the colour drained from his face. He then took to the dance floor with his wife. I don't know what he said to her but I noticed she kept glancing in my direction.

Soon the celebration party was over, so when I saw Cowley about to leave I slipped out of the club before him. When he appeared I got hold of him by his red hair and dragged him away from his wife and around the corner. He was struggling all the time but I gave him a couple of shots to the face and messed him up a bit, just as he tried to mess us up in the Old Horns public house. I really gave it to him because I knew that Ron's condition was due to the beating he had taken in the Old Horns. At this time my brother Ron's migraine was getting worse and the bouts more frequent. Sometimes he would lie in a quiet, darkened room until the pain became less. I myself have never suffered from migraine. I've had my share of headaches but never migraine, which Ron told me was much worse.

As Ron's headaches got worse, the hatred I was feeling towards Ronnie Kray was festering. But I was not alone in my hatred. Ronnie Kray had attacked another prisoner, was certified as a paranoid schizophrenic and sent to Broadmoor. Just after this I decided that I would like to visit Reggie Kray in Parkhurst. When the twins were first in prison they were allowed no visitors except for their mother. People were afraid to visit them in case they got involved with the Old Bill. It was their mother who smuggled letters out for me. Just after this another plan was set in motion that would get me inside the maximum security wing of Parkhurst to visit Reggie again and sit at the same table in the visiting room.

For many years only approved visitors were allowed in Parkhurst and I had already used the Australian migrant scam. The procedure was that after filling in the appropriate form you had to supply two passport photos. Then the local police would visit you, compare photos and submit a report to the Home Office. If you were approved, one of the passport photographs would be left at the gate at Parkhurst Prison so that when the approved visitor arrived he or she would be compared to the photograph and, if everything was in order, be allowed in for the visit. But after being thoroughly vetted by the Criminal Records Office and probably other agencies my chances of being an approved visitor were non-existent.

Our plan was simplicity itself. Among some of the prisoners who used the visiting room the passport photos were not applicable, so one of the cons named Steve Tully would send me a visiting order which enabled me to visit him, and Reggie Kray would send Debbie a visiting order. As she had been visiting him with his mother for many years and since she was a young girl she was approved. So I put the plan to Violet Kray and it was agreed that I meet her at her home with Debbie for the next Saturday visit to Reggie. Ronnie was by then in Broadmoor.

I arrived early as I like to be punctual. After a cup of tea we said our goodbyes to Charlie, the Krays' father, and set off in my Bentley. As we were leaving South London my car was stopped by the Old Bill for some feeble reason, but I believe it was because my car registration number was circulated and put on the stop and search list some time ago when the ex-Mayor of Hackney was murdered. I thought the Old Bill's play-acting had run its course so I was not expecting this. But after a bit more harassment we were allowed to resume our journey.

Of course we arrived at the prison to visit Steve Tully at the same time as Debbie was visiting Reggie Kray. We were both ushered into the same visiting rooms and I could talk to Reggie. This scheme actually worked for a couple of years. The only problem came in the shape of a screw called Butcher who when he was on duty would try to split us up. But not wanting a riot on his hands, he came to realise that it was pretty futile.

At one visit Reggie asked me not to drink before visiting him, but he's a hypocrite. He knows I'm not a drinking man, apart from the odd lager, and he seems to forget that when they were at liberty he and his twin were always drinking and taking large quantities of pills. During my visits to Reggie he would often ask me to do favours for him on the outside. On one occasion he asked me to take his current girlfriend, Christine, to a West End club for an evening. I don't recall how this situation came about but here was Reggie asking me to take his girlfriend Christine out on the town. Christine was the girl who was in bed with him when Nipper Read and his gang-busters made the dawn swoop and arrested him. I don't know what Reggie's angle was but seeing as I had to go to the West End, I took Christine with me in my Bentley to The Celebrity Club and a couple of other clubs. This was purely platonic as far as I was concerned.

Soon after Ronnie Kray was sent to Broadmoor I received a message from Reggie that Ronnie wanted to see me. Visits at Broadmoor were held in a large building that is also used for staging concerts. When he entered the visiting room I was shocked at what I saw. Believe me, I had to take a second look to be sure it was him I was seeing. I can only describe him as a shell of the man I'd last seen. He had lost several stones in weight and looked fragile. It was obvious that the clothing he was wearing was not his own. His jacket was tight and his trousers were two inches too short. He looked like some sort of witch's brother.

The visit was for two hours but I told him I could not stay too long as I had to attend to other matters. Then just as I was leaving he blurted out: 'Billy, can you do me a big favour?' Without waiting for an answer he said: 'Can you get a couple of young boys to come and see me?' I said: 'Well, I'll see', and left him there. I was anxious to get back to the car park to join my friend who had come with me but who was not keen on sitting in on the visit. That had suited me as Ronnie Kray is always suspicious about strangers.

This was the first of many spasmodic visits to Ronnie Kray over the years. I found out from him that his closest friend in Broadmoor was a young attractive fella called Charlie Smith. He also had designs on a young fella called Peter Kimble. But then, many of the patients were young boys and Ronnie must have got the hots for a lot of them. From what I know, security is so lax in Broadmoor that I can't imagine Ronnie leading a celibate life. When I saw him he always went on about boys. I did get a few boys to visit him but always at a price – I will do nothing for him without reward. In nearly all the many letters he wrote to me from Parkhurst and Broadmoor he went on about boys. In one he says: 'Do me a big favour. Can you get a boy to come and see me? He must be over 21 years old and he must have no convictions. He must also make out he knows me. Can you get two of them to visit me? The law have to go round their house so it will have to be with their parents' consent. Don't mention this in your letters. But you can write a reply and give it to my mother for me.'

There was one boy I used to tell him about and Ronnie was most anxious to meet him. He once asked me to describe the boy and I said he was about 19 years old and had blond hair cut short in the American style. After this, Ronnie sent me letters almost begging me to bring what he called 'the All-American boy' along to

Broadmoor. When I did take boys to visit him they were all disappointed with what they saw. They had expected a big monster of a man, but he looked undernourished and fragile. All the time he spoke in a whisper, as if he was frightened of being overheard, but he was never saying anything of importance. All the time his eyes were darting furtively from behind his glasses from one side of the room to the other. Later on he started a photograph album of boys and wrote asking me for pictures of 'nice boys in swimming costumes'.

When I saw him he would always ask me about things on the outside and was especially interested in hearing bad news about anyone who hadn't kept in touch with him or anyone earning big money. If I told him that one of these had been stabbed or badly beaten he would say, 'Go-oo-oo-d' – drawing the word out with full malice. He seemed to know a lot about what was going on outside. On a couple of occasions he said: 'I hear that you were in so-and-so's company in Le Hirondelle in Soho.'

He had developed a special hatred for The Bear because he had not come to visit him and had not kept in touch with Violet Kray. And yet The Bear had done two stretches of bird for him, the last being three years, at the same time as the twins had got their sentences. The Bear had never really recovered, and had come out of prison to nothing. The Krays, who could have helped him with all the money they had stashed away, gave him nothing and he ended his days in a way he didn't deserve. I used to take him out for runs in my car but he would eventually say, 'Take me home, Billy', and I would.

These visits to Ronnie became like walking on a tightrope, for he knew that I and members of my firm were collecting money from establishments that he and his brother had pioneered when they were at liberty. He'd accuse me of this and I would become indignant at the insinuations. But he was always anxious to keep friendly with me and Ron. In one letter he said, 'Bill, you are a complex character. You are like me. I am complex as well. I was happy to see you today and perhaps a bit sad as it brought back old times. Let's hope we have some happy times in the future.' This was the man who also wrote endearing letters to me asking after Ron's deteriorating health and at the same time begging me to bring him young boys to see him in Broadmoor. These letters were smuggled out to me via his mother.

I stopped visiting Ronnie because I was sick of his never-ending schemes to get near young boys. He would risk anything for these secret meetings and I suppose it was a turn-on for the youngsters who were thrilled at the idea of meeting someone as famous, despite what he was famous for. As far as I know these meetings might still be going on. So much for Broadmoor security where some of the most dangerous killers and rapists are supposed to be kept from society – at the same time as Reggie is writing to me about his concern for young men. He said in a letter to me that other cons ask him for his autograph and queue up to shake his hand. 'I feel very humble as a result and fortunate that some of the young kids here ask me how to cope with a long sentence. I hope my advice will help them because I feel sad for them.'

CHAPTER SIXTEEN

My Latter Years

Debbie had always had a passion for horses and when she was about nine or ten I took her to Taylor's Farm in nearby Cuffley, where there was a riding school. She got to love horses so much that I bought her her first pony. The pony was pretty wild in the beginning and sometimes he was very hard to catch but it seemed Debbie had a way with horses and soon she could do practically anything with him. He was named Duncan and went on to win many rosettes at the local gymkhanas. At the offset Duncan was in what they call a DIY livery, which meant Debbie would go to the stables every day to muck out, feed him and exercise him.

Eventually I found out about a few acres of land for sale in Cuffley which seemed ideal as there was a small stream nearby and also a stand-by tap. I went ahead and purchased it freehold. Shortly after buying this land I had some wooden stables erected. They were practically hidden behind trees so I never bothered to ask for planning permission – being rural, I never expected the local council to bother. But after 18 months or so the council got on to me, objected to the stables and requested that I pull them down.

I felt this was unreasonable and lodged an appeal. A couple of months later it was arranged that an official from the Ministry of Agriculture would visit the site. I found him quite reasonable and quite neutral. By this time Debbie had acquired another pony called Crystal and a horse named Cherie, who was then in foal. I pointed that out the mare was in foal and by the time she was due to give birth winter would be arriving. After some deliberation he told me there was no objection to stables, but they would have to be brick-built and the existing wooden stables would have to go. I was elated for I had in fact won the day – I had got planning permission. I lost no time on contacting an architect to draw up plans for the proposed stable development which consisted of four stables, a feed store, generator room and a soakaway. The plans were accepted by the council and the work was started.

By the time the footings for the foundations had been dug and the concrete poured in the footings, money was getting tight. As fast as I was getting it, I was spending it in solicitor's fees, architect's costs, concrete for the footings, loads of bricks and numerous other items. The project was for our children's future as later we could expand and let Debbie and my son John take in liveries. I realised they wouldn't make a fortune but at least it would be legal.

My wife had her own money in the bank so I suggested that she put some money in the project. I said that if I put her name alongside mine on the title deeds, she could see her bank manager and get an overdraft. We set up an interview and went along together to her bank manager. I had already written a list out of outgoing expenses and incoming profits. The bank manager thought it was a sound investment, as apart from the liveries I could take in our stables, Debbie was also taking in grazing in another field we rented. Three weeks after signing over half the field I owned in my wife's name, she walked out on me, Debbie and Johnny.

I felt very bitter that she would stoop to this and treat her own children in such a way. It was almost impossible for me to come to terms with. At first I thought she was putting me to the test but later I realised her younger sister was very instrumental – when I was in the slammer or in any of the clubs they were constantly together. I can honestly say I never liked my sister-in-law. She stood about four feet nothing tall and I would always refer to her as the 'poisonous dwarf' which did not go down well with her husband.

My son John had been in and out of court on assault charges and various misdemeanours time after time and it seemed that I was always in and out of court to speak up for him. But this anti-social or rebellious behaviour occurred years before my marriage started to disintegrate. I myself had been out of trouble for many years and had tried to set a good example. I have never been in the habit of having villains or any of the criminal fraternity visit me at my home but as hard as I had searched for a solution it seemed all in vain. I had tried to get through to him so much that I did not want him to finish up like me. I still don't know where I was going wrong as, no matter whether he was right or wrong, I was always at his side to speak up for him in court. But some-how I never ever found wisdom.

I remember one occasion when there was an erratic knocking on my street door. At first I thought it was the Old Bill as the rat-a-tat was all too familiar. But when I opened the door I was confronted by three guys in their twenties. I knew from their attitude they had come to sort Johnny out, but they couldn't have come to the house at a worse time and their biggest mistake was the hostile way they knocked on the street door. This on its own put me in an angry mood.

On seeing how irate I was they realised their approach had been all wrong. I screamed at them, 'What the fucking hell do you want him for? You can deal with me now!' Then I lashed out at them with a pick-axe handle I always keep behind the street door. The spokesman ducked and they all fled down the road, leaving their old jalopy outside my house. By now I was so angry I tried to wrench the car doors off but finished up whacking them with the pick-axe handle and deflating the tyres by stabbing them with a steak knife. When I left home to go to the club that night the car was still there looking like a wreck, but when I returned in the early hours of the morning it had gone, so I assume they must have towed it away.

In 1976 personal tragedy struck when I received word that John, who was at that time undergoing a sentence of Borstal training, had been rushed into Charing Cross Hospital suffering from cancer. As you can imagine, I was devastated and made my way with Debbie to Charing Cross Hospital on the Fulham Palace Road. On arrival at the ward we were asked to don plastic coveralls, put plastic covers over our shoes and masks on our faces. We found Johnny in a private ward being guarded by two guards from the Borstal.

It's so very, very difficult to describe how we felt. Everything was so clinically clean and so silent you could hear a pin drop. It seemed like I was on some huge space ship with everyone dressed in those strange overall coverings and masks. It was an eerie experience that will live with me forever. Soon we met Professor Bagshaw, Dr Newlands and the rest of the team who were kindness itself. Even though they knew John was admitted straight from Borstal they did not differentiate between patients. Within a day or so the guards were removed. John was put into a ward alongside other patients and no one was aware of his background. Debbie and I would make the journey day after day to sit in vigil at John's bedside. Every day he was getting thinner and thinner and then his hair started falling out as a result of the treatment he was receiving.

Sometimes when we would visit him in the hospital he had no appetite and we would try to get him to eat. Sometimes he got dehydrated and was put in a side ward. Every time we visited him we were expecting the worst as many young people we had seen and spoken to there had died. Although many of the patients and visitors were from different walks of life there was a bond. We were all in the same boat and all felt for each other – an experience that's very hard to explain. I could not go to a club or much else so everything was left to Ron, who was a rock.

One evening whilst I was sitting at home the telephone rang and when I answered it was Charing Cross Hospital on the line. They informed me that Johnny had walked out of the hospital. My mind was swimming! God, I thought, where can he be? The only thing I could think of was that he might make his way to the West

End, so I got in my car and made my way there, just driving round the streets hoping against hope I could find him, and praying I would not get pulled up by the Old Bill. I knew that in my state of mind I would not handle them with kid gloves. In between my search I kept phoning Debbie at home. Several hours had elapsed by now and I must have phoned Debbie and the hospital a dozen times. Finally, on the last time I phoned Debbie she told me that Johnny was in an amusement arcade at Piccadilly Circus.

I lost no time in getting there. Tears were pouring down my face when I found him. I begged him to come back to the hospital and he replied, 'Dad I can't take any more.' Finally I coaxed him to let me take him back to the hospital. Now I think, God how that boy suffered! In all John had about seven courses of drugs in between other treatments, but eventually he won the battle against the 'Big C' and was released from hospital. By now he had lost all his hair, so we decided to buy him a long-haired, hippie-style wig which was then considered fashionable by many people. Many times we would take him shopping and he sometimes became so weak he almost collapsed. I would carry him back to the car and drive him home. But in time he grew stronger. All his hair grew back and he did not have to go back to finish his Borstal sentence. In time all the anxiety and stress was behind us and I thanked God and all the hospital staff for their help in pulling him through.

Meanwhile Ron and his family were going through their own tribulations. In 1980, Ron's young daughter Kelly was killed when she was three years old by climbing underneath a milk float outside his home. While she was under it the milkman drove off and ran over her. When I heard the news of how she was killed I drove down to Epsom thinking my brother would beat the milkman to death for what he had done. But it was the opposite to all my expectations – despite Ron's grief he realised the driver of the milk float was not to blame in any way and despite his terrible ordeal and sadness he found the compassion to understand. After the tragedy the milkman packed his milk round in and started work in a factory. I think my Ron's reaction to this tragedy shows the hallmarks of a really special man, but you must draw your own conclusions. I am not saying that my brother was a saint – he was not! He had a terribly violent temper if he was provoked, but there was more good in him than bad.

Around this time and quite by chance, I was told about twelve acres of grazing land that was owned by the Co-op. For a small consideration (a backhander) I could rent it. The rent was a pittance so I took the land merely for grazing purposes for Debbie's horses so that we could give our own land a rest. Much of the 12 acres had quite a few concrete bases that greenhouses had stood on at one time. Apart from these concrete bases the land was rich in top soil, so suddenly an idea started to form in my mind and I saw that I stood a good chance of making a lot of money. Although I knew nothing about demolition or tipper work, I was well aware that tipping sites for disposing of builders' rubble were in great demand and that top soil was fetching good money. The 12-acre site was also in a perfect location off the A10. So I wrote to Broxbourne Council and told them I had rented the land and that I was keen to remove the concrete greenhouse bases and level the land in order that my daughter's horses could graze. Soon I got a reply from the Council saying they did not object.

At the time to tip a load of rubbish was costing between eight and ten pounds a load, minimum. This, plus the money the top soil was fetching, and I would be left with a real scam. All that was needed was a bulldozer. I was looking at a profit in the region of a couple of grand a week less the cost of renting a bulldozer and wages for a trusted friend or relation to run a legal scam. The only problem was that the Council would eventually put a stop to it. I told Dave Small, who employed the poisonous dwarf's husband, all about it and he offered me £5,000 to move in. Eventually he got so excited he ended up giving me £7,000 which I insisted getting in pound notes. Now the ball was in his court and he in turn passed it on for £10,000 to another two-bit firm anxious to make a killing.

The first day they opened the tip the A10 (at Cambridge Road) was congested with lorries waiting to tip their loads or buy the top soil, but within two days the law put a stop to it. I'm sure if I'd been able to put a backhander in the right hand, it would have been considered a public service.

A couple of days later two Irish guys called at my house in the hope of getting the seven grand back. I told them to go back to Dave Small. They then went on to tell me that he had repaid part of the money, to which I replied, 'Well he's the man you had the deal with, not me, so get your fucking money off him.' To this day I don't know what happened, but no one bothered to come back to me and no way would they have got a penny off me if they did. What Dave Small decided to do was no concern of mine. Maybe if they had not been so greedy they might have earned well, instead of which they got their fingers burnt because all along the A10 they put up signs saying, 'Tipping facilities available'. It was also widely advertised in many local newspapers. To me it was just a one-off business transaction.

Of course I got many begging phone calls from Dave Small, but as far as I was concerned the whole thing was just a business deal that went wrong because of them wanting to earn too much too soon. They were cry babies bawling for their money back. They knew what they were doing and surely must have been aware there was a risk. I'm sure if I had handled the situation I would not have allowed things to get out of hand. All this, of course, did not endear me to my ex-wife's sister or her husband who worked for Dave Small and who looked on Dave Small as a tin god but who was by no means above a bit of deception himself.

Violet Kray died in 1982. It was a bit of a shock, but I suppose all the travelling she had done over the years in visiting the twins was a big factor in driving her to a comparatively early grave. Debbie and I attended the funeral and joined the twins' brother, Charlie, and a select couple of dozen in a drink afterwards at a little pub next door to Braithwaite House, the block of flats where Violet and her husband lived. I felt extremely sorry for Charlie, the misused old father, as now he was on his own. He seldom had a visitor even though he was in bad shape himself. For the past few years he had become completely teetotal – and a virtual prisoner in his own council flat. I would call on him quite often but not once did I witness the presence of anyone else apart from his grandson, Gary.

Shortly after Violet Kray died I went to see Ronnie in Broadmoor and he asked how my brother Ron was doing. He then asked me if Ron would visit him. When I mentioned this to Ron he got annoyed that Ronnie Kray should suggest a visit and asked me what it was about. I told him I didn't know but said I thought it might be because his mother had died and my brother Ron knew her quite well. Next time I saw Ron he said he'd go to Broadmoor with me to visit Ronnie Kray on the next Saturday.

When we got to the visiting room we all sat with hardly a word said. Then we ordered a pot of tea which came with cups, saucers and milk jug. After some more silence, my brother picked up the teapot and said: 'Shall I be mum?' At this, Ronnie Kray gave a very long, hard look directly at Ron, who looked back intensely into Ronnie Kray's eyes. Ronnie swiftly averted this eyeballing – you could see he was getting the worst of it. The silence went on and you could have cut the atmosphere with a knife. After we had finished our tea, my brother got up and said: 'Come on, let's make a move.' When we left he was quite indifferent to Ronnie. I could see his anger and when we got in my car he said: 'Don't ever ask me to see that fucking pig again. Did you notice the way he looked at me? Who the fuck does he think he is?' He stayed angry for a long while on the drive back. After that Ron and I rarely spoke about the Krays. I don't know why Ronnie Kray was so anxious to meet my brother again or what was going through his mind on the visit.

The year after Violet died old Charlie died. Debbie and I attended the funeral but for some reason the twins never came, though I'm sure their attendance could have been arranged. I thought throughout the latter years of his life Charlie had been shabbily treated by the twins who never seemed to have a good word to say about him. I felt sorry for old Charlie – the twins treated him like dirt. At one time he was a heavy drinker but because of his ill-health he had to give it up and never moved out of the flat. I vividly remember seeing him sitting in the kitchen on a Saturday morning, cramming four ounces into a two-ounce tin that would be taken to the twins so that they would be tobacco rich – in their early days of imprisonment they had no money whatsoever.

My brother Ron started experiencing attacks of migraine more frequently and had to lay in a darkened quiet room. By now he had moved to Epsom in Surrey. He had started a building and decorating company with our stepfather Speedy and our Uncle Arthur. He had a few craftsmen on his payroll and was doing very well. At this time I was also legitimate and dealing in car and commercial vehicle tyres and inner tubes which I bought in bulk from scrap vehicle yards. Many of the commercial tyres I had re-cut and sold to haulage contractors and many hardly used private car tyres were sold to a ready market of car dealers and private individuals. The rest would be put in containers and shipped to Third World countries where the treads of the tyres would be cut into sections for making soles for sandals and shoes and the inner tubes cut into strips to make shoe-laces.

We didn't need the rackets we had built up over the years, and by 1984 our organisation was just a skeleton. Billy Welsh had long died as had 'The Eyes'. But Chang, I and a few others were still into a few clubs and spielers. I have no medical knowledge so I was in the dark about how my brother was suffering. He was insistent that the beating we took by Ronnie Kray and all the might of their firm was the main contributing factor. Many times when the pains in his head were at their height he would really slag Ronnie Kray off and say, 'That fucking pig should have been hung, drawn and quartered.' I've heard of many boxers suffering brain damage through too many blows to the head so I finally realised that this was what had happened to Ron, and a doctor eventually confirmed it.

My brother died in July 1984. I was too devastated to do much, as was my mother, so we left all the funeral arrangements to his wife, as we did all his personal belongings except for his paintings. His wife told me he could have dropped dead at any time, but I was never aware of this during his lifetime. His death was instantaneous and when he suddenly dropped dead he was laughing and joking with my son John, his stepson Barrie and a couple of our cousins. After he died his will stipulated that he wanted his ashes to be scattered on his daughter Kelly's grave. His death increased my hatred for Ronnie Kray, this raving homosexual safely locked in Broadmoor, who was the cause of my brother's death.

Of course I have lost pals who have been shot or stabbed to death, but Ron was my flesh and blood. Anyone who said anything disrespectful about him became my target for vengeance and for weeks after Ron's death I went about being anti-social to many people, causing all manner of problems as I could not handle my grief now that my brother had gone. Finally I decided I would go to Broadmoor Hospital and get my vengeance. I would have loved to have taken a blade in there but there was always the chance I would be frisked so I decided against it. All manner of things were going through my mind.

Ronnie Kray knew the hatred I felt towards him. When my brother died he was kept well informed by his cronies and hangers-on as to how I was feeling. I knew that if I used my real name to visit him in Broadmoor he would block the visit so I used the name of Houston to gain access. When I entered the visiting room he must have known why I was there for he went as white as a sheet. But before he could do anything to stop me, I steamed straight into him, a right-hander launched with all my might and venom. Within seconds the guards pounced on me and rescued him. I was dragged out screaming obscenities at him. I was then taken to an office and questioned but after a while I was allowed to leave Broadmoor.

The following day I was at home when the phone rang and a journalist was on the line asking to speak to Billy Webb. I was puzzled as to how the press had got my phone number as I was ex-directory. I soon realised the only way it could have happened was through Ronnie Kray, who is such an egomaniac he would welcome anything to keep the Kray name in the eye of the public. I admitted I was the assailant and next day an article appeared in a national newspaper claiming it was an exclusive interview with me, when in fact everything was discussed over the phone. Much was distorted as Ronnie Kray is quite adroit at distorting facts.

At this time I was running an unlicensed drinking club in

Dalston which kept me out all night. Shortly after the Broadmoor incident I arrived home from the club at eight in the morning and found a policeman standing guard at my street door where the plate glass was smashed to smithereens. Inside I found that my home was smashed to pieces. I later read in the local paper that four men had arrived knowing I would be at the club, wrecked my home and drove off in a Sherpa van. This I knew was Kray retribution – it had all their mark of *modus operandi*.

After my house had been smashed I just put it out of my mind and continued running the club in Dalston. I kept it trouble-free so we never had any aggravation from the Old Bill. We never drew attention to ourselves. The law certainly knew what was going on but never made an issue of it. A lot of our clients were London cab-drivers and although it was in a residential area not one of the neighbours ever complained. This was because most of them were unemployed and there was always a party going on somewhere.

In 1986 I was asked to look after the Brookside Club at Waltham Cross, which was a licensed disco with a snooker hall over it. It is situated in a residential area so the guvnor was anxious to keep it as quiet as possible for fear of losing his licence. I agreed subject to it not interfering with a spieler I was operating in Kilburn. So I agreed to give my services on a Friday evening which was the club's busiest night. There was plenty of aggro every Friday night and a few heads got busted. There were two bouncers named Alan and Steve who were nicknamed Laurel and Hardy. They were weightlifters but when any trouble started they were never at my back. But I soon got the place running smoothly. When I went there, there were constant fights and written on all the walls was 'Mad Ollie is out'. So I thought that this Mad Ollie, whoever he was, needed to be seen and spoken to. I found him with a couple of his yobs and within seconds I had grabbed him around the throat and said, 'What the fuck are you up to, Mad Ollie?' He cringed and said, 'What have I done?' I told him that if I saw him again I would break his back, or words to that effect. That was the last I saw of Mad Ollie.

After a while my pedigree became common knowledge to the patrons and trouble-makers, so customers I never knew at all were buying me drinks and calling me Bill or Billy and shaking hands with me. Within no time at all there was no more trouble and the club was nice and clean. During the six years I ran the Brookside Club's security I only had one good bouncer, a guy called Colin Pomfrett. The rest were just posers and rubbish. Colin Pomfrett became a good friend of mine and I have since experienced his loyalty to me in the face of any opposition. Soon it was common knowledge that I was minding the Brookside and had ousted all the local undesirables and that I could be found there on most Fridays. So friends would often drop in to have a chat. Meanwhile, and of paramount importance, I was still running my spieler in Kilburn.

Soon I was seeing quite a lot of Bobby Ramsey who at this time was minding the Manhattan Club, about a 15-minute drive from the Brookside. Bobby would begin his stint at the Manhattan at 10 p.m. and I started at 9 p.m. So it was a regular thing for Ramsey to have a drink with me at the Brookside for half an hour or so before going to the Manhattan.

My settled routine was disturbed again by the terrible news that my son John had hung himself at the age of 30. I had no idea he was in such a state that he would take his own life. He had fallen out with his mother since she had remarried and, without my knowing it, was completely isolated in his flat in Cheshunt. He had continued to be in trouble with the police and saw me as a knight in shining armour who could do anything. I asked for the inquest to be put off until I had been on a trip to America. But it was held in my absence and conveniently arranged so that the only witnesses were the police themselves.

The inquest disclosed that John was on bail following an alleged assault on a policeman at the Cheshunt Carnival. Nothing was said about the way he felt he was being harassed by the police. As could be expected, any Old Bill who had dealings with John knew all about my pedigree and no doubt passed their knowledge on to their friends and colleagues. So it was inevitable that John had been a target for the police. I heard afterwards that the coroner had said that because I had not seen my son since May of that year

I could not be aware that he was being harassed. It never entered the coroner's head that the reason I was not aware of the harassment was that for some time up to John's death we were not on speaking terms.

The funeral was perhaps the hardest of all to handle as my feelings ran high at all the hypocrisy I witnessed. It's all too soul-searching and depressing. Debbie and I looked after the funeral arrangements and a friend, Brian Nelson, and his wife, Sandra took care of the catering arrangements. I was further upset when both the Kray twins sent flowers and letters of condolence. Ronnie Kray wrote to me, 'It is at a time like this that we can forgive and forget. You forgave me once and now I am forgiving you.' Ronnie never cared about my son and I have never forgiven him for anything. He wrote this for his own reasons. People always exploit these things and if nothing else he got a mention in the local paper for his efforts.

The saddest thing about my son's tragic death is that he loved his mother so much. He was forever buying her gifts. Shortly before the tragedy there was an argument when his mother told him she was moving to Suffolk. She now lives in a £300,000 house and her son never even had a wardrobe in his flat. But these things only came to light when it was left to Debbie and I to clear his flat out. We found he was living with just the bare necessities.

I am paying the price now for allowing myself to believe the things I did. I am not making excuses for myself or passing the buck, but these are facts. John's mother couldn't care less and she never even bothered to send her own daughter a birthday card. These things are very hurtful but I must try to accept it and live with it as best I can.

I have always tried in the latter years of my life to live in obscurity but it was not to be. As soon as I moved into my present house a letter came from Reggie Kray to my daughter Debbie. Because of his unintelligible writing on the envelope the letter was not delivered to our address, but went instead to another girl named Debbie who was living in the same street. When she received the letter and saw it came from Reggie Kray she went straight to the local police station alarmed and confused. Eventually it was ironed out, but this is just one of the many things that was to happen to deny my bid for obscurity.

Even after all these years Reggie Kray still writes to express his love for my beautiful daughter, Debbie. Nobody encourages him, least of all Debbie, but like his twin he is an egomaniac. He even sent Debbie a photograph of himself when he was about 30 years of age, stressing how he regularly goes to the gym and what good shape he's in. In another of his letters to Debbie he sends his condolences at my son's suicide and in the same letter he asked her to send him a photograph of herself in a swimming suit. His letters are full of comments about what a beautiful body she has, what a lot he has to talk to her about, and how she is a major part of his plans when he gets out of prison. But Debbie is happily married now and living in a new area under her married name so there is nothing to connect her with me. She will not be going on the 'world cruise by boat' that Reggie has invited her to.

As far as Reggie is concerned he seems to be living a comfortable life in Parkhurst. When Peter Gillette was in there with him, they were known as Mr and Mrs Kray. Because the Home Office disapproved of this at one stage they moved him to Wandsworth to 'cool off'. Reggie's claims his 'love' for Gillette is platonic and Gillette told the *Sun* that Reggie and he had written a song called *Spiteful Words* about the gossip that surrounded them in Parkhurst.

As far as Ronnie's plans for the future are concerned, he hopes to open a club and call it Sweeney Todd's. There's going to be a striped barber's pole outside and for decor he plans to have a barber's chair with sawdust on the floor spattered with red ink (supposedly blood) for gory effect. Then there will be a separate section looking like a pie shop. When he described his plans for this club to me in Broadmoor he would get very excited and his eyes would bulge.

When the Krays are released they will undoubtedly try to begin where they left off, but any attempt will be short-lived as today organised crime is more streamlined and sophisticated. But nevertheless Ronnie might convince Reggie that they could indeed organise a new firm and as always Reggie might allow himself to be dominated by his twin brother and go along with any scheme just for the inner satisfaction he would achieve by pleasing him. Although it may seem preposterous, I have always believed that although the Kray twins are individuals they are both governed by the one evil brain – Ronnie enslaving Reggie, who does not have the power to resist. It is a fact that they claim to have telepathic communication with each other, and so close is their bond that since their imprisonment they write to each other every day without fail.

As for all the so-called charity they say they do, they make sure that whatever charitable act they carry out is always fully advertised. You must draw your own conclusions. As for Ronnie Kray's insatiable lusting after young boys, he's now saying he is bisexual, but this is a load of rubbish. In my experience he's one hundred per cent homosexual. I think the only solution is long gone. It's a pity they abolished the death penalty. This would have been right and just in their case and would have saved a lot of heartache and misery to many people who now can only sit and watch the glamorisation of the Krays.

Over the years of their imprisonment, due to film and media propaganda, they have an abundance of fans and a form of groupies who have been misguided into allowing themselves to be swept along by all the hype surrounding the Krays, each and every one of them hoping to get on the gravy train in the event of one of the Krays being released. And there are people like Peter Gillette and Steve Tulley who both served time in Parkhurst with Reggie, both of whom are devout followers of the Krays. Tulley was a former inmate of Parkhurst and became very close to Reggie, who looked on him like a son. Tulley was released a few years ago but wasn't out long before getting nicked and put back in the slammer for two years. He is now out again. So besotted is Tulley that since his friendship with Reggie he changed his name to Steve Tulley Kray. I'm sure there will be some future link-up – on a couple of occasions I received letters from Reggie suggesting that Steve Tulley work in conjunction with me until he and his twin were released. But for Reggie Kray to suggest such a thing is lunacy itself. I had no wish to work with the Krays and nothing would tempt me. Very few, if any, Kray followers and sympathisers ever knew the real Krays and their opinions are based on mere sentiment. The Krays have broken every law imaginable. While in Broadmoor Ronnie married two women who had begun their relationships on a pen-pal friendship with Reggie in Parkhurst. Reggie passed them on to his twin in Broadmoor who, though he is a raving homosexual, married them both.

As for my views on the establishment, I don't hold myself responsible for a multitude of things they have done to me against my will, and I certainly did not do it to myself. Maybe my feelings and views on the establishment go back to when I was a juvenile. These days it is a national pastime to follow people like the Krays and mass murderers like the Yorkshire Ripper. For English people to pretend to be surprised and nauseated at extreme violence is on a par with an old worn-out prostitute expressing her moral indignation at sex before marriage – because they are quite happy to be entertained by it.

As for my conscription into the army, that is no different than being forced into service by a press gang, which was indeed the practice many years ago. In my mind the press gang might have been the lesser of two evils – in those far-off days you did at least have a chance of receiving a share of the spoils of war. Can you imagine what it feels like to forcibly have your hair shorn off and stripped of all your dignity and never given any respect at all? Of course you can take no more and you desert. Then after a stint of freedom you're captured and returned to your regiment. Soon you find out that all or most of your kit has been stolen by your comrades in arms and 'friends'. Then the administration work out the loss and you are billed for it directly from your weekly pay, though I was never there long enough to receive much of that as I was either in detention barracks or posted as a deserter again. I am certainly not responsible for what the establishment has done to me. I have taken no part in the sins of this fucked-up, guilty country and I am only responsible for my own corrupt self.

Of course people like me will have to be a bit cautious in our everyday affairs, for among the Kray sympathisers there is a lunatic fringe. None of these people are known to me any more –

they are the morons who met the twins on a pen-pal basis. Our worst fear is the Kray mentality: 'Hurt them where it hurts most!'